WE HAVE COME THROUGH

PETER FORBES is a writer, journalist and editor. He was Editor of *Poetry Review*, Britain's leading poetry magazine, from 1986 to 2002. His anthology *Scanning the Century: The Penguin Book of the Twentieth Century in Poetry* (1999) was widely acclaimed. He translated Primo Levi's personal anthology, *The Search for Roots*, published by Penguin Press in 2001.

SURVIVORS' POETRY is a national literature and performance charity with 28 groups and more than 2500 members nationwide. Its purpose is to challenge and change the social and cultural definitions of poets and poetry, making connections between creativity and mental health. Survivors' Poetry aims to reach all survivors, including the one in four of us who will suffer from mental health problems this year. For further information, please contact Survivors' Poetry, Diorama Arts Centre, 34 Osnaburgh Street, London NW1 3ND.

We Have Come Through

100 POEMS CELEBRATING COURAGE IN
OVERCOMING DEPRESSION AND TRAUMA

edited by PETER FORBES

SURVIVORS' POETRY

BLOODAXE BOOKS

ISBN: 1 85224 619 7

First published 2003 by
Bloodaxe Books Ltd,
Highgreen,
Tarset,
Northumberland NE48 1RP
in association with
Survivors' Poetry,
Diorama Arts Centre,
34 Osnaburgh Street
London NW1 3ND.

www.bloodaxebooks.com
For further information about Bloodaxe titles
please visit our website or write to
the above address for a catalogue.

Bloodaxe Books Ltd acknowledges the financial
assistance of Arts Council England, North East.
Survivors' Poetry and its publication of this book
are supported by Arts Council England, London.

Printed in Great Britain by
Cromwell Press Ltd, Trowbridge, Wiltshire.

CONTENTS

Welcome to the Club

Aftermath and Redemption

Survival Strategies

COMING THROUGH

Jack Kerouac: '...the only people for me are the mad ones, the ones who are mad to live, mad to talk, mad to be saved, desirous of everything at the same time, the ones who never yawn or say a commonplace thing, but burn, burn, burn, like fabulous roman candles...' (*On the Road*)

John Dryden ('Absalom and Achitophel'):
  Great wits are sure to madness near allied,
  And thin partitions do their bounds divide.

Roy Porter: 'The meanings of madness are thus manifold, equivocal, and hard to interpret, but at least a substantial body of discourse exists on which to form interpretations.' (*Mind-Forged Manacles: A History of Madness in England from the Restoration to the Regency*)

R.D. Laing: 'Madness need not be all breakdown. It may also be break-through.' (*The Politics of Experience*)

Noel Malcolm: '...to write nonsense was not to express the strangeness of unconscious thought but to engage in a highly self-conscious stylistic game.' (*The Origins of English Nonsense*)

John Thompson: '...in these poems there are depths of the self that in life are not ordinarily acknowledged and in literature are usually figured in disguise.' (review of Robert Lowell's *Life Studies*)

Seamus Heaney: '...it is salutary to be able to conceive of Ó Rathaille's rawness of feeling, his partisan fury and his bare-handed single combat with the ruin of his times as a pattern of poetic fate and not entirely an aberration and deprivation.' 'The Poems of the Dispossessed Repossessed', *The Government of the Tongue*)

Adam Phillips: 'Poets, after all, are not famous for their mental health.' ('Poetry and Psychoanalysis', *Promises, Promises*)

[Quotations selected by Survivors' Poetry]

INTRODUCTION

That poetry can be a source of inspiration and solace belongs to traditional wisdom but its role has become clearer in recent years. Certain poems have always circulated in *samizdat*, to be pasted up above desks: these are the poems that seem to address you and your problems personally. To bind up a problem in a particular form of memorable words is not to solve it, but it does confer a certain power: the primitive, magical power of naming, which is at the root of all poetry.

The *samizdat* poems began to escape from their unofficial status with the coming of *Poems on the Underground* in 1986. People would notice a particularly striking poem pinned up in public, on the tube trains, and when the first anthology appeared the book was snapped up by those who wanted to have their favourites in a permanent form.

The realisation that poetry is useful had several consequences. One was a new emphasis on its therapeutic role. Survivors' Poetry was founded in 1991 to act as an umbrella for the poetry activities of people who had tangled with the mental health system at whatever level. It prospered, both nationally and locally, and today has 2500 members. Survivors' Poetry exists to help survivors come to terms with the effects of mental distress in the most creative and personally empowering ways possible.

We Have Come Through celebrates the tenth anniversary of Survivors' Poetry by drawing on poems from a very wide range of sources: from Shakespeare, Milton, Blake and John Clare, through 20th-century greats such as Hardy, Yeats, Stevie Smith, Robert Lowell, Anne Sexton and Sylvia Plath, to members of Survivors' Poetry. Poems were also commissioned for the book from poets including Sujata Bhatt, U.A. Fanthorpe, Sophie Hannah, Roger McGough and Andrew Motion.

The poems chart a journey through intimations of alienation, the causes of madness, the individual's experience at the nadir, through to healing and redemption. The final section has poems that can function as a charm against adversity.

The resilience celebrated here takes many forms: from Claudine Toutoungi's clangorous, jazzy fanfare for recovery (one of six poems in the book that came from Survivors' members) to Primo Levi writing, not directly about surviving Auschwitz, but about the vegetable persistence of his "neighbour", the chestnut tree outside his lifelong home, as an emblem for all survival. What unites all the poems is the assertion of human particularity, stubbornness and dissidence against 'mind-forged manacles', whether the mind that clamps and cramps is one's own or that of some external authority.

Especially powerful are those poems that chart the emergence of hope after despair. Poems like George Herbert's 'The Flower' convince the reader that both the despair and the alleviation were real for the writer and they hold out the promise that relief can come. The mood of resolution and defiance is one of poetry's strongest suits and in this book it ensures that a collection of poems on a grim theme can be, not depressing, but heartening.

PETER FORBES

Scenario for a Walk-on Part

I Wish

Oh I wish that there were some wing, some wing,
Under which I could hide my head,
A soft grey wing, a beautiful thing,
Oh I wish that there were such a wing,

And then I should suddenly be quite sure
As I never was before,
And fly far away, and be gay instead
Of being hesitating and filled with dread,
Oh I wish I could find a wing.

But today as I walk on the pavement I see
Where a car is parked, where a car is parked,
In the wheel's bright chromium hub I see
A world stretching out that is like but unlike
The world that encloses me.

And I wish to pass through the shining hub
And go far away, far away,
As far as I might on the wings of the dove
That first I thought would succour me
And carry me far away,
Oh the hub is my love far more than the dove
That first I thought would succour me.

And now the shining beautiful hub
Opens its door to me,
I enter, I enter, through the hub I have entered
The world that shines so bright,
The road stretches there in ochre; and blue
Is the sky I am walking into; and white
Is the beach I perceive of a heavenly sea
A-roll in the realms of light,
It rolls in the realms of light.

STEVIE SMITH (1902-71)

On the Way to the Depot

It's a pleasant night. So tonight I'll talk on the way
Of the images I seem to think in every day
Five strange years after:
Of how my life appears to me.
I don't speak of it, the thing itself, not that,
But of how I seem to see our lives in the light of it.
It's as though you live in big rooms filled with laughing;
I see little tables, and shining black pianos,
And you very busy. And me outside in the street
(Don't laugh) sweeping it.
The place I suppose is my idea of heaven.
I haven't described it (who could?)
But I've put in some writing desks and black pianos
Because that's, if I'm honest, the best my poor brain can rise to
Without inventing. Spirits, like flames, that meet
Melting into each other – yes, that makes sense to me often
But not (and you know this) every day.
Anyway, here I am
Out on the pavement. And every night
I wheel my day's collection to the depot
Where it's assessed. But
(And here's the odd part)
I don't know who does the assessing
Or what it's best to bring. One just leaves it all there
And goes to bed; every day.
The streets and dreams and faces that I've seen now
Without you. Or with you?...
It's late.
Time to turn in my collection.
Heaven knows how I'm doing!
When I sleep
Visit me then, reassure me. Don't share my puzzle.
And let me hear you laugh at my dustman's hat...

P.J. KAVANAGH (*b.* 1931)

Unpicked

I am unpicked by every wandering thing:
That stormy girl, the impermanence of May,
The things birds tell me in the tunes they sing,
The tender tumult of my children's play.
All, all unpicks my bones, unpicks my bones;
I speak in dissonances, quarter tones.

I have flown thoughts and words so far down wind
No artifice will now decoy them home;
Hung out a heart for other hearts to find.
I am a man whom speech has driven dumb,
Crushed by the simple weight of being good.
I am a stone that brims with some dark blood.

I still have craft, and I can bandage you
The wounds of long-dead poets; in my car
These distant, careful hands know what to do.
I know small histories of beast and star.
I am the scattered pages of a book
Whose theme is lost. I wear an alien look.

I know the drowning fly, the shorn dark hair,
The soldier weeping on his iron bed
In some old hutment by a windy square,
I know the unhealing sutures in my head,
I am unpicked; I cannot face alone
The vigorous, careless damage I have done.

The soft bombs drumming on my childhood make
Their crazy thunder on my dreaming ear:
I know boys' savagery, and each mistake
That I accomplish draws me into fear.
I stand reproached and into danger where
The haunted faces of my friends lie bare.

There was a time I would have laughed to see
You bend and break under my wilful hand
In some wild contest, and your misery
Had fed those vanities I understand.
Such strength was worthless. A deep amnesty
Has called those weapons home that suited me.

I am unpicked, but if you need a way
Of making such destruction doubly sure,
A mocking word or glance in casual play
Will be sufficient. I shall still endure.
Rejection I have always understood:
Her enigmatic marble face, her hood.

You whom I chose, who seem to have a need
For what a scarecrow's pockets can supply,
Take what you want, if you have skill to feed
On simple food when other horns run dry.
I will keep little back. I hang my mail
In some museum on a withered nail.

I think of old-gold castles on French hills
And all those ancient slit and tippling towers,
Their deep-set, murderous, defensive skills
Open to soft invasions from the flowers.
Does each hurt bee die lacking power to sting?
I am unpicked by every wandering thing.

PETER SCUPHAM (*b.* 1933)

15

I Am Vertical

But I would rather be horizontal.
I am not a tree with my root in the soil
Sucking up minerals and motherly love
So that each March I may gleam into leaf,
Nor am I the beauty of a garden bed
Attracting my share of Ahs and spectacularly painted,
Unknowing I must soon unpetal.
Compared with me, a tree is immortal
And a flower-head not tall, but more startling,
And I want the one's longevity and the other's daring.

Tonight, in the infinitesimal light of the stars,
The trees and flowers have been strewing their cool odors.
I walk among them, but none of them are noticing.
Sometimes I think that when I am sleeping
I must most perfectly resemble them –
Thoughts gone dim.
It is more natural to me, lying down.
Then the sky and I are in open conversation,
And I shall be useful when I lie down finally:
Then the trees may touch me for once, and the flowers have time
     for me.

SYLVIA PLATH (1932-63)

Childhood

I used to think that grown-up people chose
To have stiff backs and wrinkles round their nose,
And veins like small fat snakes on either hand,
On purpose to be grand.
Till through the banisters I watched one day
My great-aunt Etty's friend who was going away,
And how her onyx beads had come unstrung.
I saw her grope to find them as they rolled;
And then I knew that she was helplessly old,
As I was helplessly young.

FRANCES CORNFORD (1886-1960)

Scenario for a Walk-on Part

The borrowed walking-stick that makes me lame,
The single curiously worn-down tyre,
The hanging button and forgotten name,
The grinning of the vulnerable liar:
These are the gambits of a chosen game,
A well-cut personality on hire,
Mirrors too low, the eyebrows graze the frame,
Warming my hands before an unlit fire.

Dinner a skirmish, legs uncrossed and crossed,
An alp of linen and the sight of nylons,
Pudding arriving full of fruit and frost,
And, swimming in their syrup, smoking islands,
Lips at a silver spoon proclaim me lost,
My single joke counters a threat of violence.
The table cleared, I cannot count the cost
Of dinner or of nerves. The rest is silence.

Now in the sharpest lock at close of day,
Hands as if manacled, the gravel spurting,
My hosts with linked arms waving me away,
The gulf of what I didn't say still hurting
(Since you are only known by what you say),
Yawning beneath my silent murmur skirting
The dangerous excuse, the wish to stay,
Like the evasions of protracted flirting:

Alone I drive away with my awareness
That once again I've failed the magic word
Whose demon locks me up inside my bareness,
The charming openness unsaid, unheard.
Is love the better for its hurts and rareness?
I frown and think so. Falling into third
On a hill, I glimpse a face: the sheer unfairness
Fights with my sense of shame at being stirred.

The sexy minister reclaims his scarf,
A girl in denim runs to meet a train,
Mrs Jocasta bastes the fatted calf,
The guests have taken to their beds again:
I hold the floor but nobody will laugh,
No one is there to kiss if I complain,
I enter only in the second half,
Unwilling, underwritten, used to pain.

JOHN FULLER (*b.* 1937)

Wants

Beyond all this, the wish to be alone:
However the sky grows dark with invitation-cards
However we follow the printed directions of sex
However the family is photographed under the flagstaff –
Beyond all this, the wish to be alone.

Beneath it all, desire of oblivion runs:
Despite the artful tensions of the calendar,
The life insurance, the tabled fertility rites,
The costly aversion of the eyes from death –
Beneath it all, desire of oblivion runs.

PHILIP LARKIN (1922-85)

The Death of Poetry

The fallen leaves this morning
are in a silly mood.
Dancing and leapfrogging
they chase each other down the road.

No, that's not true.
Leaves don't have moods,
Unable to dance or play organised games,
what you see is merely dead matter.

Then it's the wind bringing them to life!
Full of mischief, it races along the pavement
tugging at scarves, knocking off hats,
whistling as it goes.

No, that's not true either.
The wind doesn't have feelings. Inanimate,
it's a force of nature, as simple as that.
Wind is just air on the move.

Then it must be the sun smiling down on us!
Or the moon!
Yes, the moon knows all our secrets,
dreaming in her star-filled chamber.

Boiling gas. Frozen rock.
Put away your pen. Close your book.

ROGER McGOUGH (*b.* 1937)

Blues on the Tube

Ever thought of riding the rapids on the tube,
just for the hell of it, to keep yourself amused,
hopping on and off, going with the flow,
no place you've got to be, nowhere to go?
Ever tried to balance, to let go of the rail,
to stand up at stations and learn how to sail,
then jumped from the fish bowl and stared back in
at each gaping mouth and redundant limb?
Ever cruised the network just for the thrill?
Mental Illness Need Not Mean You're Mentally Ill.
Ever read that poster? Ever lost the thread,
or felt thoughts speeding up, like trains inside your head?
Ever tried to get back home, but felt too confused?
That's Circle Line jaundice, Piccadilly Line blues.

SARAH WARDLE (*b.* 1969)

Walking Around

It happens that I am tired of being a man.
It happens that I go into the tailor's shops and the movies
all shrivelled up, impenetrable, like a felt swan
navigating on a water of origin and ash.

The smell of barber shops makes me sob out loud.
I want nothing but the repose either of stones or of wool,
I want to see no more establishments, no more gardens,
nor merchandise, nor glasses, nor elevators.

It happens that I am tired of my feet and my nails
and my hair and my shadow.
It happens that I am tired of being a man.

Just the same it would be delicious
to scare a notary with a cut lily
or knock a nun stone dead with one blow of an ear.
It would be beautiful
to go through the streets with a green knife
shouting until I died of cold.

I do not want to go on being a root in the dark,
hesitating, stretched out, shivering with dreams,
downwards, in the wet tripe of the earth,
soaking it up and thinking, eating every day.

1 do not want to be the inheritor of so many misfortunes.
I do not want to continue as a root and as a tomb,
as a solitary tunnel, as a cellar full of corpses,
stiff with cold, dying with pain.

For this reason Monday burns like oil
at the sight of me arriving with my jail-face,
and it howls in passing like a wounded wheel,
and its footsteps towards nightfall are filled with hot blood.

And it shoves me along to certain corners, to certain damp houses,
to hospitals where the bones come out of the windows,
to certain cobblers' shops smelling of vinegar,
to streets horrendous as crevices.

There are birds the colour of sulphur, and horrible intestines
hanging from the doors of the houses which I hate,
there are forgotten sets of teeth in a coffee-pot,
there are mirrors
which should have wept with shame and horror,
there are umbrellas all over the place, and poisons, and navels.

I stride along with calm, with eyes, with shoes,
with fury, with forgetfulness,
I pass, I cross offices and stores full of orthopaedic appliances,
and courtyards hung with clothes on wires,
underpants, towels and shirts which weep
slow dirty tears.

PABLO NERUDA (1904-73)
translated from the Spanish by W.S. Merwin.

The Sash Window

Outside that house, I stood like a dog;
The window was mysterious, with its big, dull pane
Where the mud pastes are thrown by dark, alkaline skies
That glide slowly along, keeping close to the ground.

– But for the raging disgust which shook me
So that my throat was scratched by her acid
(Whose taste is the true Latin of culture) –
I could have lived the life of these roads.

That piece of filthy laurel moves up and down,
And then the dead rose-leaves with their spat-on look
Where the sour carbon lies...under
The sash of the window comes the smell of stewing innards,

With the freshly washed lavatory – I know where
The old linoleum has its platinum wet patches
And the disinfectant dries off in whiffs.
Hellish, abominable house where I have been young!

With your insane furnishings – above all
The backs of dressing-tables where the dredged wood
Faces the street, raw. And the window
With its servant-maid's mystery, which contains *nothing*,

Where I bowed over the ruled-up music books
With their vitreous pencilling, and the piano keys
That touched water. How forlornly my strong, destructive head
Eats again the reek of the sash window.

ROSEMARY TONKS (*b.* 1932)

Dolor

I have known the inexorable sadness of pencils,
Neat in their boxes, dolor of pad and paper-weight,
All the misery of manilla folders and mucilage,
Desolation in immaculate public places,
Lonely reception room, lavatory, switchboard,
The unalterable pathos of basin and pitcher,
Ritual of multigraph, paper-clip, comma,
Endless duplication of lives and objects.
And I have seen dust from the walls of institutions,
Finer than flour, alive, more dangerous than silica,
Sift, almost invisible, through long afternoons of tedium,
Dropping a fine film on nails and delicate eyebrows,
Glazing the pale hair, the duplicate grey standard faces.

THEODORE ROETHKE (1908-63)

Unplayed Music

We stand apart in the crowd that slaps its filled glasses
on the green piano, quivering her shut heart.
The tavern, hung with bottles, winks and sways
like a little ship, smuggling its soul through darkness.
There is an arm flung jokily round my shoulders,
and clouds of words and smoke thicken between us.
I watch you watching me. All else is blindness.

Outside the long street glimmers pearl.
Our revellers' heat steams into the cold
as fresh snow, crisping and slithering
underfoot, witches us back to childhood.
Oh night of ice and Schnapps, moonshine and stars,
how lightly two of us have fallen in step
behind the crowd! The shadowy white landscape
gathers our few words into its secret.

All night in the small grey room
I'm listening for you, for the new music
waiting only to be played; all night I hear nothing
but wind over the snow, my own heart beating.

CAROL RUMENS (*b.* 1944)

Sonnet XIX

When I consider how my light is spent
  Ere half my days in this dark world and wide,
  And that one talent which is death to hide
  Lodged with me useless, though my soul more bent
To serve therewith my maker, and present
  My true account, lest he returning chide,
  'Doth God exact day-labour, light denied?'
  I fondly ask. But Patience, to prevent
That murmur, soon replies, 'God doth not need
  Either man's work or his own gifts; who best
  Bear his mild yoke, they serve him best: his state
Is kingly. Thousands at his bidding speed,
  And post o'er land and ocean without rest;
  They also serve who only stand and wait.'

JOHN MILTON (1608-74)

I Am

I am: yet what I am none cares or knows
  My friends forsake me like a memory lost,
I am the self-consumer of my woes –
  They rise and vanish in oblivious host,
Like shadows in love's frenzied stifled throes: –
And yet I am, and live – like vapours tost

Into the nothingness of scorn and noise,
  Into the living sea of waking dreams,
Where there is neither sense of life or joys.
  But the vast shipwreck of my life's esteems;
Even the dearest, that I love the best,
Are strange – nay, rather stranger than the rest.

I long for scenes, where man hath never trod,
  A place where woman never smiled or wept –
There to abide with my Creator, God,
  And sleep as I in childhood sweetly slept,
Untroubling, and untroubled where I lie,
The grass below – above the vaulted sky.

JOHN CLARE (1793-1864)

Wessex Heights

There are some heights in Wessex, shaped as if by a kindly hand
For thinking, dreaming, dying on, and at crises when I stand,
Say, on Ingpen Beacon eastward, or on Wylls-Neck westwardly,
I seem where I was before my birth, and after death may be.

In the lowlands I have no comrade, not even the lone man's friend –
Her who suffereth long and is kind; accepts what he is too weak to mend:
Down there they are dubious and askance; there nobody thinks as I,
But mind-chains do not clank where one's next neighbour is the sky.

In the towns I am tracked by phantoms having weird detective ways –
Shadows of beings who fellowed with myself of earlier days:
They hang about at places, and they say harsh heavy things –
Men with a wintry sneer, and women with tart disparagings.

Down there I seem to be false to myself, my simple self that was,
And is not now, and I see him watching, wondering what crass cause
Can have merged him into such a strange continuator as this,
Who yet has something in common with himself, my chrysalis.

I cannot go to the great grey Plain; there's a figure against the moon,
Nobody sees it but I, and it makes my breast beat out of tune;
I cannot go to the tall-spired town, being barred by the forms now passed
For everybody but me, in whose long vision they stand there fast.

There's a ghost at Yell'ham Bottom chiding loud at the fall of the night,
There's a ghost in Froom-side Vale, thin-lipped and vague, in a shroud
            of white,
There is one in the railway train whenever I do not want it near,
I see its profile against the pane, saying what I would not hear.

As for one rare fair woman, I am now but a thought of hers,
I enter her mind and another thought succeeds me that she prefers;
Yet my love for her in its fulness she herself even did not know;
Well, time cures hearts of tenderness, and now I can let her go.

So I am found on Ingpen Beacon, or on Wylls-Neck to the west.
Or else on homely Bulbarrow, or little Pilsdon Crest,
Where men have never cared to haunt, nor women have walked with me,
And ghosts then keep their distance: and I know some liberty.

THOMAS HARDY (1840-1928)

The Morning Star

The man who lives alone gets up while the sea's still dark
and the stars waver. A warm breeze
rises over the sea and the shore,
softening the air. This is the time when nothing
can happen. Even the pipe between his teeth
hangs empty. He bathes quickly at night.
Already he's lit a big fire of branches
and watches it redden the ground. Even the sea
will soon be blazing like the fire.

There's nothing more bitter than starting a day
when nothing will happen. Nothing more bitter
than uselessness. A greenish star,
surprised by dawn, hangs tired in the sky.
It sees the still-dark sea and the glow of the fire,
where the man warms his hands for the sake of doing something;
it looks on and falls asleep between the sombre mountains
with their bed of snow. The slowness of time
is unrelenting for someone who expects nothing.

Is it worth the sun's rising from the sea
and the long day's beginning? Tomorrow
the lukewarm dawn and transparent light will return,
it will be like yesterday and nothing will ever happen.
The man who lives alone would like only to sleep.
When the last star fades from the sky
he slowly fills and lights his pipe.

CESARE PAVESE (1908-50)
translated from the Italian by Margaret Crosland

FROM Hamlet

How weary, stale, flat, and unprofitable
Seems to me all the uses of this world!
Fye on 't! O fye! 'tis an unweeded garden,
That grows to seed; things rank, and gross in nature,
Possess it merely. That it should come to this!

WILLIAM SHAKESPEARE (1564-1616)

The Feeling

One has a feeling it is all coming to an end;
no, not that. One has a feeling it is like
that war whose last battle was fought long
after the treaty was signed. The imminence
relates to a past doom. We look back
to one time, some time, something that already has
happened. Look, we are still here, but note
that nothing of moment has happened for an age, an age,
for as long as we can piece together, not
since the time it happened. Was there that time?
Once, there must have been. When will it end?

WILLIAM BRONK (1918-99)

Why We Go Mad

The Way

There is the world, we say, and mean a kind
of mechanism, big machine that stands
there mornings when we come on. We check the gauge
and pull a lever we learned to pull, and wait,
and stuff comes out. We put stuff in. And wait.
Nights, we go home and rest. After a while of this,
we stop; and, mornings, someone else comes on.

This is a way we made to look at things.
The way is always there, you can bank on that,
though the flow of the slot is fuller here or there
or it dwindles away. We scheme then, over moves
to make more stuff come out, or a trick technique
to overlay whole sections like a new
machine, devise a way: it works somehow.

These changes are written down: what ones were made
and who served where and when – how many days.
It makes it seem more real except that real
is what it doesn't seem at all: the skips
at night, the end a blank. What went wrong?
It isn't the way things are, but only a way
we made to look at things, among various ways.

It has rewards: the pellets of food we get
are the soothing boon of problems and problems solved
because they were solvable. We grasp at that.
We wish it might be so who sleep and die
– do what we call those names, not knowing what
we do, yet wanting a life outside the one
that sleeping drifts towards, death illuminates.

WILLIAM BRONK (1918-99)

Neurosis

I am a dark cypress driven in the wind,
And the quarrelling voices of children behind
The Sunday streets. I am the listener, waiting
In doorways for the sounds of struggle
And torment. I am the shock machine in the empty ward,
And the enemy soldier under the point of the sword.
I am a little boy crying out Dolore in his sleep,
And the dazed women in rusty black who weep
Outside provincial cemeteries, and a foetus taken piecemeal
From its mother, and an old woman dying
Of cancer in a back room. I am my own analyst lying
Dead in his bed with the marks of the syringe
Like a macabre tattoo on his white body.

In childhood I was the red lady of my own nightmares,
And the pursuing jeers, and the hostile stares.
I was Manuela dead in a German courtyard, and the open maw
Of the butcher boy's basket, and the threat of war.
I was the clinging Goodwins who sucked down the merry
Cricketers, and the drums at the tattoo, and the poisoned berry.
Did you see me lingering at the gates of Buchenwald,
Or running from Electra, or making friends with the bald
Syphilitic hawking laces on the sea-front?
I was all men collecting the dole in long lines
In bitter weather, and the accident siren shrieking from the mines.
You have heard my name called in the courts
Of law for perversion and murder, and malice aforethought.

Would you know me? I am also a young woman, growing
My flowers in season, feeding my cats, knowing
Little, but feeling everything, writing at all times
And in all places, working out rhythms and rhymes.
I make clothes for young children, a red kilt
Or a jacket for a newly-delivered child,
Assuaging my envy and covering my guilt.
Sometimes, from my husband's arms, I catch
A glimpse of the potency of love, like a mirage
Soon gone, and I wonder if I shall ever be whole,
Or always playing torturer and tortured in my double role.

ELIZABETH BARTLETT (*b.* 1924)

London

I wander through each chartered street
Near where the chartered Thames does flow,
And mark in every face I meet
Marks of weakness, marks of woe.

In every cry of every man,
In every infant's cry of fear,
In every voice, in every ban,
The mind-forged manacles I hear –

How the chimney-sweeper's cry
Every blackening church appalls,
And the hapless soldier's sigh
Runs in blood down palace walls;

But most through midnight streets I hear
How the youthful harlot's curse
Blasts the new-born infant's tear
And blights with plagues the marriage hearse.

WILLIAM BLAKE (1757-1827)

Report on Experience

I have been young, and now am not too old;
And I have seen the righteous forsaken,
His health, his honour and his quality taken.
    This is not what we were formerly told.

I have seen a green country, useful to the race,
Knocked silly with guns and mines, its villages vanished,
Even the last rat and the last kestrel banished –
    God bless us all, this was peculiar grace.

I knew Seraphina; Nature gave her hue,
Glance, sympathy, note, like one from Eden.
I saw her smile warp, heard her lyric deaden;
    She turned to harlotry; – this I took to be new.

Say what you will, our God sees how they run.
These disillusions are His curious proving
That He loves humanity and will go on loving;
    Over there are faith, life, virtue in the sun.

EDMUND BLUNDEN (1896-1974)

A Prayer to George Herbert

Dead priest of a missionary art
   Each verse seems like a host
Dipt in wine lifted to God's heart
        Who sits apart
From angels to catch your utmost cry,
   Which must pierce Him like a dart.

I too am moved to inwards tears by your
   Simple heart-wrenching rhymes
And if you hear this from the floor
        Of Heaven, pour
Down your love and blessings: my crimes,
   My sins give me no peace, but war.

JOHN O'DONOGHUE (*b.* 1958)

To You

This was written just before my one and only breakdown, as a personal note to my wife Celia to explain what was running through my head in hobnail boots. I thought it was a very private poem. But then I took the risk of reading it in public and found that it always brought a special response, there were always people, not necessarily my generation, who'd been through similar troubles. What I thought was one of my most personal poems became one of my most public, especially when Peter Schat the Dutch composer set it to music and performed it in concert.

Later my fear of madness receded until nowadays it stands at only number 29 on my hit list of Fears.

One: we were swaddled, ugly-beautiful and drunk on milk.
Two: cuddled in arms always covered by laundered sleeves.
Three: we got sand and water to exercise our imaginative faculties.
Four: we were hit. Suddenly hit.

Five: we were fed to the educational system limited.
Six: worried by the strange creatures in our heads, we strangled
some of them.
Seven: we graduated in shame.
Eight: World War Two and we hated the Germans as much as
our secret bodies, loved the Americans as much as the Russians,
hated killing, loved killing, depending on the language in the
Bible in the breast pocket of the dead soldier, we were crazy-
thirsty for Winston Superman, for Jesus with his infinite tommy-
gun and the holy Spitfires, while the Jap dwarfs hacked through
the undergrowth of our nightmares – there were pits full of
people-meat – and the real bombs came, but they didn't hit us
my love, they didn't hit us exactly.
My love, they are trying to drive us mad.

So we got to numbers eight, nine, ten, and eleven,
growing scales over every part of our bodies,
Especially our eyes.

Because scales were being worn, because scales were armour.
And now we stand, past thirty, together, madder than ever.
We make a few diamonds and lose them.
We sell our crap by the ton.
My love, they are trying to drive us mad.

Make love. We must make love
Instead of making money.
You know about rejection? Hit. Suddenly hit.
Want to spend my life building poems in which untamed
People and animals walk around freely, lie down freely
Make love freely
In the deep loving carpets, stars circulating in their ceilings,
Poems like honeymoon planetariums.
But our time is burning.
My love, they are trying to drive us mad.

Peace was all I ever wanted.
It was too expensive.
My love, they are trying to drive us mad.

Half the people I love are shrinking.
My love, they are trying to drive us mad.

Half the people I love are exploding.
My love, they are trying to drive us mad.

I am afraid of going mad

ADRIAN MITCHELL (*b.* 1932)

Hatred

See how efficient it still is,
how it keeps itself in shape –
our century's hatred.
How easily it vaults the tallest obstacles.
How rapidly it pounces, tracks us down.

It's not like other feelings.
At once both older and younger.
It gives birth itself to the reasons
that give it life.
When it sleeps, it's never eternal rest.
And sleeplessness won't sap its strength; it feeds it.

One religion or another –
whatever gets it ready, in position.
One fatherland or another
whatever helps it get a running start.
Justice also works well at the outset
until hate gets its own momentum going.
Hatred. Hatred.
Its face twisted in a grimace
of erotic ecstasy.

Oh these other feelings,
listless weaklings.
Since when does brotherhood
draw crowds?
Has compassion
ever finished first?
Does doubt ever really rouse the rabble?
Only hatred has just what it takes.

Gifted, diligent, hardworking.
Need we mention all the songs it has composed?
All the pages it has added to our history books?
All the human carpets it has spread
over countless city squares and football fields?

Let's face it:
it knows how to make beauty.
The splendid fire-glow in midnight skies.
Magnificent bursting bombs in rosy dawns.
You can't deny the inspiring pathos of ruins
and a certain bawdy humour to be found
in the sturdy column jutting from their midst.

Hatred is a master of contrast –
between explosions and dead quiet,
red blood and white snow.
Above all, it never tires
of its leitmotif – the impeccable executioner
towering over its soiled victim.

It's always ready for new challenges.
If it has to wait awhile, it will.
They say it's blind. Blind?
It has a sniper's keen sight
and gazes unflinchingly at the future
as only it can.

WISLAWA SZYMBORSKA (*b.* 1923)
translated from the Polish by Stanislaw Baranczak and Clare Cavanagh

The Little Cardboard Suitcase

Events pushed me into this corner;
I live in a fixed routine,
With my cardboard attaché case full of rotting books.
...If only I could trust my blood! Those damn foreign women
Have a lot to answer for, marrying into the family –

– The mistakes, the wrong people, the half-baked ideas,
And their beastly comments on everything. Foul.
But irresistibly amusing, that is the whole trouble.

With my cardboard suitcase full of occidental literature
I reached this corner, to educate myself
Against the sort of future they flung into my blood –
The events, the people, the ideas – the *ideas*!
And I alone know how disreputable and foreign.

But as a thinker, as a professional water-cabbage,
From my desk, of course, I shall dissolve events
As if they were of no importance...none whatever.

...And those women are to blame!
I was already half-way into my disreputable future,
When I found that they had thrown into my blood
With the mistakes, the people, the ideas (ideas indeed!)
This little cardboard suitcase...damned
Beloved women...and these books, opium, beef, God,

At my desk (lit by its intellectual cabbage-light)
I found them – and they are irresistibly amusing –
These thoughts that have been thrown into my blood.

ROSEMARY TONKS (*b.* 1932)

Why Should Not Old Men Be Mad?

Why should not old men be mad?
Some have known a likely lad
That had a sound fly-fisher's wrist
Turn to a drunken journalist;
A girl that knew all Dante once
Live to bear children to a dunce;
A Helen of social welfare dream,
Climb on a wagonette to scream.
Some think it a matter of course that chance
Should starve good men and bad advance,
That if their neighbours figured plain,
As though upon a lighted screen,
No single story would they find
Of an unbroken happy mind,
A finish worthy of the start.
Young men know nothing of this sort,
Observant old men know it well;
And when they know what old books tell,
And that no better can be had,
Know why an old man should be mad.

W.B.YEATS (1865-1939)

Penguins

The protective instinct among the Emperor penguins
(Adolf Remane, *Das soziale Leben der Tiere*)
Attains monstrous dimensions:
It reaches a point where one nestling
Is looked after by dozens of parents

The drive to hatch the eggs
And to warm and feed the nestlings
(Observed and described by Adolf Portmann and Sapin-Jaloustre)
Is all-powerful for the Emperor penguins
The impulse for possession and care of the nestling
Is so strong among these birds
That the natural historian Wilson calls it most pathetic:

...As soon as the nestling leaves the brood-fold on
the abdomen of the adult bird or is abandoned by it,
a compact throng of excited penguins appears...
These are birds without progeny who want to
appropriate the nestling...Converging on the
nestling, and furiously pecking away at each other,
each adult bird attempts to set it on its feet, to keep it
from being exposed on the ice...

Their love is touching
And relentless
During this violent adoption
The young are wounded
Some of them fall
Others try to escape
They squeeze into cracks in the ice
And prefer to freeze or starve to death
Rather than suffer that terrible affection
That murderous excess of care

The ornithologist Schuz once overhead a young penguin crying out
        in despair:
Why wasn't I born a stork?
Mother would eat me by mistake
And I could have some peace

ARTUR MIEDZYRZECKI (*b.* 1922)
translated from the Polish by Arthur Miedzyrzecki and John Batki

FROM **Howl**

What sphinx of cement and aluminum bashed open their skulls and
     ate up their brains and imagination?
Moloch! Solitude! Filth! Ugliness! Ashcans and unobtainable dollars!
     Children screaming under the stairs! Boys sobbing in armies!
     Old men weeping in the parks!
Moloch! Moloch! Nightmare of Moloch! Moloch the loveless! Mental
     Moloch! Moloch the heavy judger of men!
Moloch the incomprehensible prison! Moloch the crossbone soulless
     jailhouse and Congress of sorrows! Moloch whose buildings
     are judgment! Moloch the vast stone of war! Moloch the
     stunned governments!
Moloch whose mind is pure machinery! Moloch whose blood is
     running money! Moloch whose fingers are ten armies!
     Moloch whose breast is a cannibal dynamo! Moloch whose
     ear is a smoking tomb!
Moloch whose eyes are a thousand blind windows! Moloch whose
     skyscrapers stand in the long streets like endless Jehovahs!
     Moloch whose factories dream and croak in the fog! Moloch
     whose smoke-stacks and antennae crown the cities!
Moloch whose love is endless oil and stone! Moloch whose soul is
     electricity and banks! Moloch whose poverty is the specter
     of genius! Moloch whose fate is a cloud of sexless hydrogen!
     Moloch whose name is the Mind!
Moloch in whom I sit lonely! Moloch in whom I dream Angels!
     Crazy in Moloch! Cocksucker in Moloch! Lacklove and
     manless in Moloch!
Moloch who entered my soul early! Moloch in whom I am a con-
     sciousness without a body! Moloch who frightened me out
     of my natural ecstasy! Moloch whom I abandon! Wake up
     in Moloch! Light streaming out of the sky!
Moloch! Moloch! Robot apartments! invisible suburbs! skeleton
     treasuries! blind capitals! demonic industries! spectral nations!
     invincible madhouses! granite cocks! monstrous bombs!
They broke their backs lifting Moloch to Heaven! Pavements, trees,
     radios, tons! lifting the city to Heaven which exists and is
     everywhere about us!
Visions! omens! hallucinations! miracles! ecstasies! gone down the
     American river!

Dreams! adorations! illuminations! religions! the whole boatload of
   sensitive bullshit!
Breakthroughs! over the river! flips and crucifixions! gone down the
   flood! Highs! Epiphanies! Despairs! Ten years' animal
   screams and suicides! Minds! New loves! Mad generation!
   down on the rocks of Time!
Real holy laughter in the river! They saw it all! the wild eyes! the
   holy yells! They bade farewell! They jumped off the roof!
   to solitude! waving! carrying flowers! Down to the river!
   into the street!

ALLEN GINSBERG (1926-97)

Spiritual Chickens

A man eats a chicken every day for lunch,
and each day the ghost of another chicken
joins the crowd in the dining room. If he could
only see them! Hundreds and hundreds of spiritual
chickens, sitting on chairs, tables, covering
the floor, jammed shoulder to shoulder. At last
there is no more space and one of the chickens
is popped back across the spiritual plain to the earthly.
The man is in the process of picking his teeth.
Suddenly there's a chicken at the end of the table,
strutting back and forth, not looking at the man
but knowing he is there, as is the way with chickens.
The man makes a grab for the chicken but his hand
passes right through her. He tries to hit the chicken
with a chair and the chair passes through her.
He calls in his wife but she can see nothing.
This is his own private chicken, even if he
fails to recognise her. How is he to know
this is a chicken he ate seven years ago
on a hot and steamy Wednesday in July,
with a little tarragon, a little sour cream?
The man grows afraid. He runs out of his house
flapping his arms and making peculiar hops
until the authorities take him away for a cure.
Faced with the choice between something odd
in the world or something broken in his head,
he opts for the broken head. Certainly,
this is safer than putting his opinions
in jeopardy. Much better to think he had
imagined it, that he had made it happen.
Meanwhile, the chicken struts back and forth
at the end of the table. Here she was, jammed in
with the ghosts of six thousand dead hens, when
suddenly she has the whole place to herself.
Even the nervous man has disappeared. If she
had a brain, she would think she had caused it.
She would grow vain, egotistical, she would
look for someone to fight, but being a chicken
she can just enjoy it and make little squawks,

silent to all except the man who ate her,
who is far off banging his head against a wall
like someone trying to repair a leaky vessel,
making certain that nothing unpleasant gets in
or nothing of value falls out. How happy
he would have been to be born a chicken,
to be of good use to his fellow creatures
and rich in companionship after death.
As it is he is constantly being squeezed
between the world and his idea of the world.
Better to have a broken head – why surrender
his corner on truth? – better just to go crazy.

STEPHEN DOBYNS (*b.* 1941)

To Carry the Child

To carry the child into adult life
Is good? I say it is not,
To carry the child into adult life
Is to be handicapped.

The child in adult life is defenceless
And if he is grown-up, knows it,
And the grown-up looks at the childish part
And despises it.

The child, too, despises the clever grown-up,
The man-of-the-world, the frozen,
For the child has the tears alive on his cheek
And the man has none of them.

As the child has colours, and the man sees no
Colours or anything,
Being easy only in things of the mind,
The child is easy in feeling.

Easy in feeling, easily excessive
And in excess powerful,
For instance, if you do not speak to the child
He will make trouble.

You would say a man had the upper hand
Of the child, if a child survive,
I say the child has fingers of strength
To strangle the man alive.

Oh it is not happy, it is never happy,
To carry the child into adulthood,
Let children lie down before full growth
And die in their infanthood
And be guilty of no man's blood.

But oh the poor child, the poor child, what can he do,
Trapped in a grown-up carapace,
But peer outside of his prison room
With the eye of an anarchist?

STEVIE SMITH (1902-71)

FROM The Book of Disquiet

It's one of those days when the monotony of everything oppresses me like being thrown into jail. The monotony of everything is merely the monotony of myself, however. Each face, even if seen just yesterday, is different today, because today isn't yesterday. Each day is the day it is, and there was never another one like it in the world. Only our soul makes the identification – a genuinely felt but erroneous identification – by which everything becomes similar and simplified. The world is a set of distinct things with varied edges, but if we're near-sighted, it's a continual and indecipherable fog.

I feel like fleeing. Like fleeing from what I know, fleeing from what's mine, fleeing from what I love. I want to depart, not for impossible Indias or for the great islands south of everything, but for any place at all – village or wilderness – that isn't this place. I want to stop seeing these unchanging faces, this routine, these days. I want to rest, far removed, from my inveterate feigning. I want to feel sleep come to me as life, not as rest. A cabin on the seashore or even a cave in a rocky mountainside could give me this, but my will, unfortunately, cannot.

Slavery is the law of life, and it is the only law, for it must be observed: there is no revolt possible, no way to escape it. Some are born slaves, others become slaves, and still others are forced to accept slavery. Our faint-hearted love of freedom – which, if we had it, we would all reject, unable to get used to it – is proof of how ingrained our slavery is. I myself, having just said that I'd like a cabin or a cave where I could be free from the monotony of everything, which is the monotony of me – would I dare set out for this cabin or cave, knowing from experience that the monotony, since it stems from me, will always be with me? I myself, suffocating from where I am and because I am – where would I breathe easier, if the sickness is in my lungs rather than in the things that surround me? I myself, who long for pure sunlight and open country, for the ocean in plain view and the unbroken horizon – could I get used to my new bed, the food, not having to descend eight flights of stairs to the street, not entering the tobacco shop on the corner, not saying good-morning to the barber standing outside his shop?

Everything that surrounds us becomes part of us, infiltrating our physical sensations and our feeling of life, and like spittle of the great Spider it subtly binds us to whatever is close, tucking us into a soft bed of slow death which is rocked by the wind. Everything is us, and we are everything, but what good is this, if everything is nothing? A ray of sunlight, a cloud whose shadow tells us it is passing, a breeze that rises, the silence that follows when it ceases, one or another face, a few voices, the incidental laughter of the girls who are talking, and then night with the meaningless, fractured hieroglyphs of the stars.

FERNANDO PESSOA (1888-1935)
translated from the Portuguese by Richard Zenith

My own Heart let me more have Pity on

My own heart let me more have pity on; let
Me live to my sad self hereafter kind,
Charitable; not live this tormented mind
With this tormented mind tormenting yet.
   I cast for comfort I can no more get
By groping round my comfortless, than blind
Eyes in their dark can day or thirst can find
Thirst's all-in-all in all a world of wet.

Soul, self; come, poor Jackself, I do advise
You, jaded, let be; call off thoughts awhile
Elsewhere; leave comfort root-room; let joy size
At God knows when to God knows what; whose smile
's not wrung, see you; unforeseen times rather – as skies
Betweenpie mountains – lights a lovely mile.

GERARD MANLEY HOPKINS (1844-89)

To Himself

Now you will rest, tired heart, forever. Finished
Is your last fantasy, which I felt sure
Would endure forever. It's finished. I know in my bones
That hope and even desire are cold
For any more fond illusions.
Stay easy forever. You've been
Throbbing long enough. Nothing is worth
This beating and beating; the earth doesn't
Deserve a sigh. Life is nothing
But blankness of spirit, a bitter taste, and the world
Mud. Now rest in peace. Despair
For the last time. Fate gave our kind
No gift but death. Cast a cold eye now
On yourself, on nature, on that hideous hidden force
That drives all things to their destruction,
And the infinite *all is vanity* of it all.

GIACOMO LEOPARDI (1798-1837)
translated from the Italian by Eamonn Grennan

Halves

I am going to rip myself down the middle into two pieces
because there is something in me that is neither
the right half nor the left half nor between them.
It is what I see when I close my eyes, and what I see.

As in this room there is something neither ceiling
nor floor, not space, light, heat or even
the deep skies of pictures, but something that beats softly
against others when they're here and others not here,

that leans on me like a woman,
curls up in my lap and walks
with me to the kitchen or out of the house altogether
to the street – I don't feel it, but it beats and beats;

so my life: there is this, neither before me
nor after, not up, down, backwards nor forwards from me.
It is like the dense, sensory petals in a breast
that sway and touch back. It is like the mouth of a season,

the cool speculations bricks murmur, the shriek in orange,
and though it is neither true nor false, it tells me
that it is quietly here, and, like a creature, is in pain;
that when I ripen it will crack open the locks, it will love me.

C.K.WILLIAMS (*b.* 1936)

Welcome to the Club

Depression

You lie, snail-like, on your stomach –
I dare not speak or touch,
Knowing too well the ways of our kind –
The retreat, the narrowing spiral.

We are both convinced it is impossible
To close the distance.
I can no more cross this room
Than Zeno's arrow.

WENDY COPE (*b.* 1945)

Her Kind

I have gone out, a possessed witch,
haunting the black air, braver at night;
dreaming evil, I have done my hitch
over the plain houses, light by light:
lonely thing, twelve-fingered, out of mind.
A woman like that is not a woman, quite.
I have been her kind.

I have found the warm caves in the woods,
filled them with skillets, carvings, shelves,
closets, silks, innumerable goods;
fixed the suppers for the worms and the elves:
whining, rearranging the disaligned.
A woman like that is misunderstood.
I have been her kind.

I have ridden in your cart, driver,
waved my nude arms at villages going by,
learning the last bright routes, survivor
where your flames still bite my thigh
and my ribs crack where your wheels wind.
A woman like that is not ashamed to die.
I have been her kind.

ANNE SEXTON (1928-74)

FROM A Season in Hell

Long ago, if my memory serves me, my life was a banquet where everyone's heart was generous, and where all wines flowed.

One evening I pulled Beauty down on my knees. I found her embittered and I cursed her.

I took arms against justice.

I ran away. O witches, poverty, hate – I have confided my treasure to you!

I was able to expel from my mind all human hope. On every form of joy, in order to strangle it, I pounced stealthily like a wild animal.

I called to my executioners to let me bite the ends of their guns, as I died. I called to all plagues to stifle me with sand and blood. Disaster was my god. I stretched out in mud. I dried myself in criminal air. I played clever tricks on insanity.

Spring brought to me an idiot's terrifying laughter.

But recently, on the verge of giving my last croak, I thought of looking for the key to the ancient banquet where I might possibly recover my appetite.

Charity is the key. This lofty thought proves I dreamt it!

ARTHUR RIMBAUD (1854-91)
translated from the French by Wallace Fowlie

Join the Club

Flashing my neurotic's badge I dare them
to ask me for my licence. I don't look
much different from the rest of them –
in fact, a certain calm emanates.
I've seen and felt so much I'm like
a bird on a withered tree, singing.

Diagnosis proclaims me not psychotic.
Sensitive and shy, this patient
has symptoms of depression with a touch
of anxiety and agoraphobia.
We're not supposed to read our files,
but just the same, we do.
It's really quite interesting
the way the doctors size us up,
and there's a preening of feathers,
and comparing of notes.
Sensitive and shy sounds quite genteel,
as opposed to schizoid, paranoid
and abusive, anorexic, manic,
or simply mad.

I'm really quite presentable – not that
you could take me anywhere - I tend
to shiver and sweat in open spaces.
Still, I only suffer from a disease
as common as a cold, ubiquitous
as birds on withered trees, singing.

Poetry as therapy is not quite acceptable.
Myself, I find it more effective
than valium. It's just that if
the literary world took us too seriously
we'd be out on our necks, and ours,
like Anne Boleyn's, are extremely slender,
even if the executioner is very expert.

We are a clean and well-behaved lot,
don't need a leper's bell,
but keep our badges polished
just in case we recognise our kind.
I'm introspective. What are you?
Oh, me, comes the reply. I'm just a bird
on a withered tree, singing.

ELIZABETH BARTLETT (*b*. 1924)

We're through

The fairground mirrors of the mind
that fatten us for the kill or slimmer still
afloat like balloons from spools that unwind
we hover on a knife's edge or dance on a hill

Dizzy or busy Lizzies are we, loved at first
left soon to the ring of Loopy Lous
next, Crazy or Lazy, Jane or Maisie cursed
talking too much or sitting too much for you

Before you know it we're hosting a tea party
mad as hatters with seats to spare drawing
conclusions and treacle-wells out of curiosity
no Alices or angels at the table daring, staring

Eyes only seeking magical wonders from our
fairground memories to garnish their tasteless lives,
the sips of sour, hospital tea. Matrix-blind they tour
around our mirrors, careless words and thoughts connive,

Tripping over their fears, closed to the mirrors
we can't switch off, conniving to get the fairground view
but dodge the fare – this is not for the faint-hearted of you
we're through and have left you behind, we're through with you.

ANNA MENMUIR (b. 1962)

Psyche

Yesterday life was faster and fuller than this,
when I arrived here, barefoot, with clenched fist,
ready to kick and punch. Yes, I fought.
Having travelled the earth to find him, I was distraught,
seeking him who came to me divinely in the night,
always in darkness, invisible, so that it might
all have been a dream, but one I believed.

I journeyed here, hoping to be received
in this, his house, his palace, his temple,
with him at the top of the aisle by the oracle,
extending his hand like a bridegroom. It was a trick.
I tried to escape, ran down corridors, looked for an exit,
like Theseus without Ariadne's thread.

It was no good. I was surrounded,
trapped like an animal caught in the nets. I'd be fed
to the Minotaur, or to one of the heads
of the Hydra. By fighting I only made matters worse:
seven sentries appeared, where before was one nurse.

I climbed on the couches, knocked over a chair,
hid in an alcove to block out the glare
of a light. Cupid was nowhere. The voices of my sisters screamed,
'He's not your lover! He's a monster!' In a living dream
I'd become Odysseus in the Cyclops' cave,
about to be swallowed with no chance of being saved.

They said *No One* would hurt me, but I guessed their game:
I knew that *No One* was *Somebody*'s name.
They sharpened a needle for the eye of my mind,
speared it in, till I felt myself fade and go blind,
freefalling into a blackened abyss,
forever shut out from the day, like Oedipus.

Then I turned into Sisyphus pushing a rock,
as I struggled to keep awake, to swim back to the top.
Next I was Aeneas in Hades, the nurses were ghosts.
I was Psyche again when I awoke.

This room is silent now. On the door is a number
in washable ink. I wear a hospital toga.
When the nurse comes in with more drugs, she will say
in a mocking tone, 'How is Aeneas today?'
Yes, yesterday with racing thoughts and clenched fist,
I can say life was faster and fuller than this.

SARAH WARDLE (*b.* 1969)

Every lovely Limb's a Desolation

I feel a mortal isolation
Wrap each lovely limb in desolation,
Sight, hearing, all
Suffer a fall.

I see the pretty fields and streams, I hear
Beasts calling and birds singing, oh not clear
But as a prisoner
Who in a train doth pass
And through the glass
Peer;
Ah me, so far away is joy, so near.

Break, break the glass, you say?
These thoughts are but a mood
Blow them away, go free?
They are my whole soul's food.

Ghost's food! Sepulchral aliment!
Thou sleekst in me Death's tegument
And so art bent
To do, and this I know.

Yet there are days, oh brief,
When thought's caught half-asleep
(Most merrily) and drowsing
Set in a meadow browsing.

Ah then, like summer breeze in lovely trees
That comes in little pants unequally,
Or like the little waves of summer seas
That push and fuss
In heaven knows what sort of busyness,
Idly, idly, my thoughts bring me to sleep,
On sunny summer day, to sleep. In sun
I fall asleep.

But I must wake and wake again in pain
Crying – to see where sun was once all dust and stain
As on a window pane –

All, all is isolation
And every lovely limb's a desolation.

STEVIE SMITH (1902-71)

FROM Hamlet

HAMLET. Lady, shall I lie in your lap? (*Lying down at* OPHELIA's *feet*).
OPHELIA. No, my lord.
HAMLET. I mean, my head upon your lap?
OPHELIA. Ay, my lord.
HAMLET. Do you think I meant country matters?
OPHELIA. I think nothing, my lord.
HAMLET. That's a fair thought to lie between maids' legs.
OPHELIA. What is, my lord?
HAMLET. Nothing.
OPHELIA. You are merry, my lord.
HAMLET. Who, I?
OPHELIA. Ay, my lord.
HAMLET. O God! your only jig-maker. What should a man do, but be merry? for, look you, how cheerfully my mother looks, and my father died within these two hours.
OPHELIA. Nay, 'tis twice two months, my lord.
HAMLET. So long? Nay, then, let the devil wear black, for I'll have a suit of sables. O heavens! die two months ago, and not forgotten yet? Then there's hope a great man's memory may outlive his life half a year: But, by'r-lady, he must build churches then: or else shall he suffer not thinking on, with the hobby-horse, whose epitaph is, For, O, for, O, the hobby-horse is forgot.

WILLIAM SHAKESPEARE (1564-1616)

FROM Jubilate Agno

Let Luke rejoice with the Trout – Blessed be Jesus in Aa, in Dee
and in Isis.
*For the Skrew, Axle and Wheel, Pulleys, the Lever and inclined
Plane are known in the Schools.*

Let Cosam rejoice with the Perch, who is a little tyrant, because
he is not liable to that, which he inflicts.
*For the Centre is not known but by the application of the members to
matter.*

Let Levi rejoice with the Pike – God be merciful to all dumb
creatures in respect of pain.
For I have shown the Vis Inertiae to be false, and such is all nonsense.

Let Melchi rejoice with the Char, who cheweth the cud.
For the Centre is the hold of the Spirit upon the matter in hand.

Let Joanna rejoice with the Anchovy – I beheld and lo! a great
multitude!
*For FRICTION is inevitable because the Universe is FULL of God's
works.*

Let Neri rejoice with the Keeling Fish who is also called the
Stock Fish.
For the PERPETUAL MOTION is in all the works of Almighty GOD.

Let Janna rejoice with the Pilchard – the Lord restore the seed of
Abishai.
*For it is not so in the engines of man, which are made of dead
materials, neither indeed can be.*

Let Esli rejoice with the Soal, who is flat and spackles for the
increase of motion.
*For the Moment of bodies, as it is used, is a false term – bless God ye
Speakers on the Fifth of November.*

Let Nagge rejoice with the Perriwinkle – 'for the rain it raineth
every day.'
For Time and Weight are by their several estimates.

Let Anna rejoice with the Porpus, who is a joyous fish and of good omen.

For I bless GOD in the discovery of the LONGITUDE direct by the means of GLADWICK.

Let Phanuel rejoice with the Shrimp, which is the children's fishery.

For the motion of the PENDULUM is the longest in that it parries resistance.

Let Chuza rejoice with the Sea-Bear, who is full of sagacity and prank.

For the WEDDING GARMENTS of all men are prepared in the SUN against the day of acceptation.

Let Susanna rejoice with the Lamprey, who is an eel with a title.

For the Wedding Garments of all women are prepared in the MOON against the day of their purification.

Let Candace rejoice with the Craw-fish – How hath the Christian minister renowned the Queen.

For CHASTITY is the key of knowledge as in Esdras, Sir Isaac Newton and now, God be praised, in me.

CHRISTOPHER SMART (1722-71)

Last Day

There is a day a dreadfull day
Still following the past
When sun and moon are passed away
And mingle with the blast
There is a vision in my eye
A vacuum o'er my mind
Sometimes as on the sea I lye
Mid roaring waves and wind

When valleys rise to mountain-waves
And mountains sink to seas
When towns and cities temples graves
All vanish like a breeze
The skys that was are past and o'er
That almanack of days
Year-chronicles are kept no more
Oblivion's ruin pays

Pays in destruction, shades, and hell
Sin goes in darkness down
And therein sulphur's shadows dwell
Worth wins and wears the crown
The very shore, if shore I see,
All shrivelled to a scroll
The Heavens rend away from me
And thunder's sulphurs roll

Black as the deadly thunder-cloud
The stars shall turn to dun
And heaven by that darkness bowed
Shall make day's light be done
When stars and skys shall all decay
And earth no more shall be
When heaven itself shall pass away
Then thou'lt remember me

JOHN CLARE (1793-1864)

FROM Dream Songs

54

'NO VISITORS' I thumb the roller to
and leans against the door.
Comfortable in my horseblanket
I prop on the costly bed & dream of my wife,
my first wife,
and my second wife & my son.

Insulting, they put guardrails up,
as if it were a crib!
I growl at the head nurse; we compose on one.
I have been operating from *nothing*,
like a dog after its tail
more slowly, losing altitude.

Nitid. They are shooting me full of sings.
I give no rules. Write as short as you can,
in order, of what matters.
I think of my beloved poet
Issa & his father who
sat down on the grass and took leave of each other.

147

Henry's mind grew blacker the more he thought.
He looked onto the world like the act of an aged whore.
Delmore, Delmore.
He flung to pieces and they hit the floor.
Nothing was true but what Marcus Aurelius taught,
'All that is foul smell & blood in a bag.'

He lookt on the world like the leavings of a hag.
Almost his love died from him, any more.
His mother & William
were vivid in the same mail Delmore died.
The world is lunatic. This is the last ride.
Delmore, Delmore.

High in the summer branches the poet sang.
His throat ached, and he could sing no more.
All ears closed
across the heights where Delmore & Gertrude sprang
so long ago, in the goodness of which it was composed
Delmore, Delmore!

JOHN BERRYMAN (1914-72)

There Is a Man

There is a man who has swept or rubbed a floor
This morning crying in the Most Holy Name
Of God for pity, and has not been able to claim
A moment's respite, that for one hour, or more.
But can the not-conceiving heart outside
Believe the atmosphere that hangs so heavy
And clouds the torment. Afterwards in the leavy
And fresher air other torments may abide,
Or pass; and new pain; but this memory
Will not pass, it is too bad and the grinding
Remains, and what is better is the finding
Of any ease from working or changing free
Words between words, and cadences in change.
But the pain is in thought, which will not freely range.

IVOR GURNEY (1890-1937)

Mental Ward

They shall be new at the roots of their sane trees
After the various drugs to ward off disaster,
They shall drift down like birds from the high fells
To the boles of the trees where no one is a stranger.

They shall celebrate their union with each other,
Men and women, speechless in life, dumb as the roots of trees,
In good communion of talk and laughter
And prove they are found now who had lost their ways.

For these are those who in the parish of living,
Having no good instrument on which to play,
Still worked hard and with the almost nothing
Of their scant tongue and brain on the great symphony.

The man who barked like a dog shall talk of angels.
The girl so far gone, no skill could disinter
Her buried soul, in superb parabolas
Of dance and song celebrate the life in her.

There shall be no more desolation or crying anywhere.

For the great pianist who strummed on one string
With a broken finger, shall have an infinity of chords,
And the stopped poet who could only say 'Good morning',
Reap with his tongue a harvest of meaningful words.

They shall be written in the centre of the page
Who were in parenthesis here,
For withdrawn from the body which held them in close siege
There shall be no more desolation anywhere.

No more desolation anywhere.

THOMAS BLACKBURN (1916-77)

award for bravery

the smelltaste of corridors and fingernails.
sounds of lino coughing, rings grating
on metal rails and nurses' legs swishing busy.
the shiny thermos looks innocuous,
unstoppered becomes theatrical.
foams smoke in slovenly huffs across his desk.

the sniffing poker waitresses chink china prickly
with roses – teacups with ornate handles my Da'
can't even get his pinky through. he is in the grip
of broderie anglais, hiding his steel-capped boots,
eyeing our cakes – pushy on their EPNS stand –
all sponge fuff and hundreds & thousands.

the tiny serviette perches – useful as origami –
on his oilstained lap. he sneaks a keek
at the permed ladies buzzing with brittle chatter
and hooked pinkies and then digs in,
wielding his cakefork like a torque wrench.
leaning over to pour, a fairy cake welds itself to his breast.

he grins across at me – conspiratorial.
cream and crumbs clot his tobacco teeth,
he clutches the mock Spode in the grime-map of his hands,
the same greasy contours that cradled me
as the Doctor's dry ice sizzle-gouged
my verruca-studded feet.

CHAR MARCH (*b.* 1961)

You, Doctor Martin

You, Doctor Martin, walk
from breakfast to madness. Late August,
I speed through the antiseptic tunnel
　　　where the moving dead still talk
of pushing their bones against the thrust
of cure. And I am queen of this summer hotel
　　　or the laughing bee on a stalk

of death. We stand in broken
lines and wait while they unlock
the door and count us at the frozen gates
　　　of dinner. The shibboleth is spoken
and we move to gravy in our smock
of smiles. We chew in rows, our plates
　　　scratch and whine like chalk

in school. There are no knives
for cutting your throat. I make
moccasins all morning. At first my hands
　　　kept empty, unraveled for the lives
they used to work. Now I learn to take
them back, each angry finger that demands
　　　I mend what another will break

tomorrow. Of course, I love you;
you lean above the plastic sky,
god of our block, prince of all the foxes.
　　　The breaking crowns are new
that Jack wore. Your third eye
moves among us and lights the separate boxes
　　　where we sleep or cry.

What large children we are
here. All over I grow most tall
in the best ward. Your business is people,
　　　you call at the madhouse, an oracular
eye in our nest. Out in the hall
the intercom pages you. You twist in the pull
　　　of the foxy children who fall

like floods of life in frost.
And we are magic talking to itself,
noisy and alone. I am queen of all my sins
forgotten. Am I still lost?
Once I was beautiful. Now I am myself,
counting this row and that row of moccasins
waiting on the silent shelf.

ANNE SEXTON (1928-74)

Walking in the Blue

The night attendant, a B.U. sophomore,
rouses from the mare's-nest of his drowsy head
propped on *The Meaning of Meaning*.
He catwalks down our corridor.
Azure day
makes my agonised blue window bleaker.
Crows maunder on the petrified fairway.
Absence! My heart grows tense
as though a harpoon were sparring for the kill.
(This is the house for the 'mentally ill'.)

What use is my sense of humour?
I grin at 'Stanley', now sunk in his sixties,
once a Harvard all-American fullback,
(if such were possible!)
still hoarding the build of a boy in his twenties,
as be soaks, a ramrod
with the muscle of a seal
in his long tub,
vaguely urinous from the Victorian plumbing.
A kingly granite profile in a crimson golf-cap,
worn all day, all night,
he thinks only of his figure,
of slimming on sherbet and ginger ale –
more cut off from words than a seal.

This is the way day breaks in Bowditch Hall at McLean's;
the hooded night lights bring out 'Bobbie',
Porcellian '29,
a replica of Louis XVI
without the wig –
redolent and roly-poly as a sperm whale,
as he swashbuckles about in his birthday suit
and horses at chairs.

These victorious figures of bravado ossified young.

In between the limits of day,
hours and hours go by under the crew haircuts
and slightly too little nonsensical bachelor twinkle
of the Roman Catholic attendants.
(There are no Mayflower
screwballs in the Catholic Church.)

After a hearty New England breakfast,
I weigh two hundred pounds
this morning. Cock of the walk,
I strut in my turtle-necked French sailor's jersey
before the metal shaving mirrors,
and see the shaky future grow familiar
in the pinched, indigenous faces
of these thoroughbred mental cases,
twice my age and half my weight.
We are all old-timers,
each of us holds a locked razor.

ROBERT LOWELL (1917-77)

Visits to St Elizabeths

This is the house of Bedlam.

This is the man
that lies in the house of Bedlam.

This is the time
of the tragic man
that lies in the house of Bedlam.

This is a wristwatch
telling the time
of the talkative man
that lies in the house of Bedlam.

This is a sailor
wearing the watch
that tells the time
of the honored man
that lies in the house of Bedlam.

This is the roadstead all of board
reached by the sailor
wearing the watch
that tells the time
of the old, brave man
that lies in the house of Bedlam.

These are the years and the walls of the ward,
the winds and clouds of the sea of board
sailed by the sailor
wearing the watch
that tells the time
of the cranky man
that lies in the house of Bedlam.

This is a Jew in a newspaper hat
that dances weeping down the ward
over the creaking sea of board
beyond the sailor

winding his watch
that tells the time
of the cruel man
that lies in the house of Bedlam.

This is a world of books gone flat.
This is a Jew in a newspaper hat
that dances weeping down the ward
over the creaking sea of board
of the batty sailor
that winds his watch
that tells the time
of the busy man
that lies in the house of Bedlam.

This is a boy that pats the floor
to see if the world is there, is flat,
for the widowed Jew in the newspaper hat
that dances weeping down the ward
waltzing the length of a weaving board
by the silent sailor
that hears his watch
that ticks the time
of the tedious man
that lies in the house of Bedlam.

These are the years and the walls and the door
that shut on a boy that pats the floor
to feel if the world is there and flat.
This is a Jew in a newspaper hat
that dances joyfully down the ward
into the parting seas of board
past the staring sailor
that shakes his watch
that tells the time
of the poet, the man
that lies in the house of Bedlam.

This is the soldier home from the war.
These are the years and the walls and the door
that shut on a boy that pats the floor
to see if the world is round or flat.

This is a Jew in a newspaper hat
that dances carefully down the ward,
walking the plank of a coffin board
with the crazy sailor
that shows his watch
that tells the time
of the wretched man
that lies in the house of Bedlam.

ELIZABETH BISHOP (1911-79)

Counting the Mad

This one was put in a jacket,
This one was sent home,
This one was given bread and meat
But would eat none,
And this one cried No No No No
All day long.

This one looked at the window
As though it were a wall,
This one saw things that were not there,
This one things that were,
And this one cried No No No No
All day long.

This one thought himself a bird,
This one a dog,
And this one thought himself a man,
An ordinary man,
And cried and cried No No No No
All day long.

DONALD JUSTICE (*b.* 1925)

Lullaby

It is a summer evening.
The yellow moths sag
against the locked screens
and the faded curtains
suck over the window sills
and from another building
a goat calls in his dreams.
This is the TV parlor
in the best ward at Bedlam.
The night nurse is passing
out the evening pills.
She walks on two erasers,
padding by us one by one.

My sleeping pill is white.
It is a splendid pearl;
it floats me out of myself,
my stung skin as alien
as a loose bolt of cloth.
I will ignore the bed.
I am linen on a shelf.
Let the others moan in secret;
let each lost butterfly
go home. Old woolen head,
take me like a yellow moth
while the goat calls hush-
a-bye.

ANNE SEXTON (1928-74)

The Passing Cloud
(from The Royal Bethlehem Hospital)

I thought as I lay on my bed one night, I am only a passing cloud
And I wiped the tear from my sorrowful eye and merrily cried aloud
Oh the love of the Lord is a fearful thing and the love of the Lord is
     mine
And what do I care for the sins of men and the tears of our guilty
     time
I will sail my cloud in the bright blue sky, in the bright blue sky I sail
And I look at the sea so merrily swung in the path of the Arctic
     whale
On the tropic belt of the uttermost wild the sea rings a merry peal
And the fish leaps up and the sharks pursue in Creation's happy reel
Oh I dance on my cloud and I cry aloud to the careless creative gust
That made us all and made the fish and the ocean that holds them fast
Hurrah hurrah for the grand old heavenly gusty creator Lord
Who said to Job, Don't bother me son, I'll do as I please my word.
Oh never was happiness like to mine as I pelt along on my cloud
In the sky-blue path of the high winds' breath, no wonder I cry aloud
With joy I cried and my cheeks were wet and the air was a singing
     space
And I thought as we shot to the upper reach, My lord, it's a lick of
     a pace.
When we swept out of sight of the troublesome earth, was I afraid,
     oh no,
I was glad to see the parochial thing pack up its traps and go
And now I go round and round I go in the merry abyss of the sky
Piercing the grand primaeval dust of the stars in their infancy
I tunnel, I burrow, I offer my dust as a dust for creation's choice
And in the ding-dong of the universe I pipe my innocent voice
I pipe my innocent voice I pipe, I pipe and I also sing
Till I'd sung too loud and woke myself up and that is another thing,
Oh I woke with a bump and they brought me here to Bethlehem's
     Royal precincts
And do I care? Not I, not I, I have shed all careful instincts,
I will laugh and sing, or be dumb if they please, and await at the
     Lord's discretion
The day I'll be one, as one I'll be, in an infinite regression
One, ha ha, with a merry ha ha, skip the fish and amoeba where are
     we now?

We are very far out, in a rarified place, with the thin thin dust in
    a giddy chase,
The dust of Continuous Creation, and how is that for
    identification?
You'll like it; you must, you know,
That merry dust does jig so.

STEVIE SMITH (1902-71)

Therapy

Did you hear the one about the shrink
who let obsessive-compulsives clean his house
as if their illnesses were his?
They made good caretakers, stayed up all night
rattling doorknobs, testing locks,
domesticated poltergeists.

He started an amateur dramatics group
with the psychotics, who had a ball
in togas, till they burnt down the hall.
Chronic depressives are always apart,
so he'd check them through his telescope,
placed them in poses from classical art

and, of course, they'd hardly ever move,
added a certain style to the grounds.
He recorded Tourette patients' sounds,
sold them to pop groups as backing tracks.
Whenever possible, he'd encourage love
between staff and patients. He had a knack

with manics, whom he sent out to shop
for all his parties, gave tarot cards
to schizoids so they could read their stars.
Perhaps he was flip with other people's pain
but his patients loved him and his hope
that two or three madnesses might make one sane.

GWYNETH LEWIS (*b.* 1959)

Aftermath and Redemption

Into the Hour

I have come into the hour of a white healing.
Grief's surgery is over and I wear
The scar of my remorse and of my feeling.

I have come into a sudden sunlit hour
When ghosts are scared to corners. I have come
Into the time when grief begins to flower

Into a new love. It had filled my room
Long before I recognised it. Now
I speak its name. Grief finds its good way home.

The apple-blossom's handsome on the bough
And Paradise spreads round. I touch its grass,
I want to celebrate but don't know how.

I need not speak though everyone I pass
Stares at me kindly. I would put my hand
Into their hands. Now I have lost my loss

In some way I may later understand.
I hear the singing of the summer grass.
And love, I find, has no considered end,

Nor is it subject to the wilderness
Which follows death. I am not traitor to
A person or a memory. I trace

Behind that love another which is running
Around, ahead. I need not ask its meaning.

ELIZABETH JENNINGS (1926-2001)

I, The Survivor

I know of course: it's simply luck
That I've survived so many friends. But last night in a dream
I heard those friends say of me: 'Survival of the fittest'
And I hated myself.

BERTOLT BRECHT (1898-1956)
translated from the German by John Willett

Beyond Decoration

Stalled, in the middle of a rented room,
The couple who own it quarrelling in the yard
Outside, about which shade of *Snowcem*
They should use. (From the bed I'd heard
Her say she liked me in my dressing-gown
And heard her husband's grunt of irritation.
Some ladies like sad men who are alone.)
But I am stalled, and sad is not the word.
Go out I cannot, nor can I stay in,
Becalmed mid-carpet, breathless, on the road
To nowhere and the road has petered out.
This was twenty years ago, and bad as that.
I must have moved at last, for I knelt down,
Which I had not before, nor thought I should.
It would not be exact to say I prayed;
What for? The one I wanted there was dead.
All I could do was kneel and so I did.
At once I entered dark so vast and warm
I wondered it could fit inside the room
When I looked round. The road I had to walk down
Was still there. From that moment it was mean
Beyond my strength to doubt what I had seen:
A heat at the heart of dark, so plainly shown,
A bowl, of two cupped hands, in which a pain
That filled a room could be engulfed and drown
And yet, for truth is in the bowl, remain...

P.J. KAVANAGH (*b.* 1931)

The Middle of Nowhere

Then the train stopped
without warning or reason
and each of us shrank
in the shell of ourselves,

turned to the window-view
chance had allotted us –
mine the quinced junk-field
where plonked on the mud-

slide shore of a flood-pond:
this black metal desk chair.
I reasoned I'd owned it
some dim pre-existence,

when I was the monarch
of trolleys and car-doors,
burst cases and suit-wrecks.
Now it just gaped there

to show me my kingdom
could not do without me,
preserving its rain-pitted
focus of blankness,

catching in sun-gleams
that version of purity
reached by dead things
with no further to fall,

and bound to persist
at the squiffed edge of vision
through all the time left
of my exile in plenty.

ANDREW MOTION (*b.* 1952)

The Journey

One day you finally knew
what you had to do, and began,
though the voices around you
kept shouting
their bad advice –
though the whole house
began to tremble
and you felt the old tug
at your ankles.
'Mend my life!'
each voice cried.
But you didn't stop.
You knew what you had to do,
though the wind pried
with its stiff fingers
at the very foundations,
though their melancholy
was terrible.
It was already late
enough, and a wild night,
and the road full of fallen
branches and stones.
But little by little,
as you left their voices behind,
the stars began to burn
through the sheets of clouds,
and there was a new voice
which you slowly
recognised as your own,
that kept you company
as you strode deeper and deeper
into the world,
determined to do
the only thing you could do –
determined to save
the only life you could save.

MARY OLIVER (*b.* 1935)

Beginning

The T-wave was abnormal
On the graph of my heart
I do not despair
It was, as it were
Just waving to you
In acknowledgement
I had thought perhaps
'If you licked my heart
It would poison you'
(A phrase borrowed
From a Holocaust survivor)
A pretentious melodramatic
Psychotic sentiment you say
Maybe so – how could I say or know
Except how it seems to me
If my heart still waves
(In psychiatric parlance
'Wobbly throw')
There is still hope for us all
Whose hearts are bruised and broken
We are not broken beyond repair
If our hearts still wave
If only on an ECG.

SARAH CAVILL (*b.* 1938)

FROM Hymn to the Supreme Being, On Recovery from a Dangerous Fit of Illness

But, O immortals! What had I to plead
   When death stood o'er me with his threat'ning lance,
When reason left me in the time of need,
   And sense was lost in terror or in trance,
My sick'ning soul was with my blood inflam'd,
And the celestial image sunk, defac'd and maim'd.

I sent back memory, in heedful guise,
   To search the records of preceding years;
Home, like the raven to the ark, she flies,
   Croaking bad tidings to my trembling ears.
O Sun, again that thy retreat was made,
And threw my follies back into the friendly shade!

But who are they, that bid affliction cease! –
   Redemption and forgiveness, heavenly sounds!
Behold the dove that brings the branch of peace,
   Behold the balm that heals the gaping wounds –
Vengeance divine's by penitence supprest –
She struggles with the angel, conquers, and is blest.

Yet hold, presumption, nor too fondly climb,
   And thou too hold, O horrible despair!
In man humility's alone sublime,
   Who diffidently hopes he's Christ's own care –
O all-sufficient Lamb! in death's dread hour
Thy merits who shall slight, or who can doubt thy power?

But soul-rejoicing health again returns,
   The blood meanders gently in each vein,
The lamp of life renew'd with vigour burns,
   And exil'd reason takes her seat again –
Brisk leaps the heart, the mind's at large once more,
To love, to praise, to bless, to wonder and adore.

The virtuous partner of my nuptial bands,
    Appear'd a widow to my frantic sight;
My little prattlers lifting up their hands,
    Beckon me back to them, to life, and light;
I come, ye spotless sweets! I come again,
Nor have your tears been shed, nor have ye knelt in vain.

CHRISTOPHER SMART (1722-71)

Discharged

The house was still – white sheets beyond the window
muffled sound
from the street outside. A glasslike chill
clarified his mind – the silence around
making him quiet and spacious

cool as a breeze.

He envisioned paper aeroplanes
dipping inside a perspex dome
from the intricate girders of which a trapeze
swung idly easy...

home

He crouched,
mouthing the word in the hall
and pressed his ear to the door as if to hear
the falling snow fall.

COLIN ROWBOTHAM (1949-2000)

Chorus of the Rescued

We, the rescued,
From whose hollow bones death had begun to whittle his flutes,
And on whose sinews he had already stroked his bow –
Our bodies continue to lament
With their mutilated music.
We, the rescued,
The nooses wound for our necks still dangle
before us in the blue air –
Hourglasses still fill with our dripping blood.
We, the rescued,
The worms of fear still feed on us.
Our constellation is buried in dust.
We, the rescued,
Beg you:
Show us your sun, but gradually.
Lead us from star to star, step by step.
Be gentle when you teach us to live again.
Lest the song of a bird,
Or a pail being filled at the well,
Let our badly sealed pain burst forth again
and carry us away –
We beg you:
Do not show us an angry dog, not yet –
It could be, it could be
That we will dissolve into dust –
Dissolve into dust before your eyes.
For what binds our fabric together?
We whose breath vacated us,
Whose soul fled to Him out of that midnight
Long before our bodies were rescued
Into the ark of the moment.
We, the rescued,
We press your hand
We look into your eye –
But all that binds us together now is leave-taking,
The leave-taking in the dust
Binds us together with you.

NELLY SACHS (1891-1970)
translated from the German by Michael Roloff

Losing and Finding

You had been searching quietly through the house
That late afternoon, Easter Saturday,
And a good day to be out of doors. But no,
I was reading in a north room. You knocked
On my door once only, despite the dark green notice,
'Do not disturb'. I went at once and found you,

Paler than usual, not smiling. You just said
'I've lost them'. That went a long way back
To running, screaming through a shop and knocking
Against giants. 'I haven't had lunch,' you said.
I hadn't much food and the shop was closed for Easter
But I found two apples and washed them both for you.

Then we went across the road, not hand in hand.
I was wary of that. You might have hated it
And anyway you were talking and I told you
About the river not far off, how some people
Swam there on a day like this. And how good the grass
Smelt as we walked to the Recreation Ground.

You were lively now as I spun you lying flat,
Talking fast when I pushed you on the swing,
Bold on the chute but obedient when, to your question
About walking up without hands, I said 'Don't. You'll fall.'
I kept thinking of your being lost, not crying,
But the sense of loss ran through me all the time

You were chatting away, I wanted to keep you safe,
Not know fear, be curious, love people
As you showed me when you jumped on my lap one evening,
Hugged me and kissed me hard. I could not keep you
Like that, contained in your joy, showing your need
As I wished *I* could. There was something elegiac

Simply because this whole thing was direct,
Chance, too, that you had found me when your parents
So strangely disappeared. There was enchantment
In the emptiness of that playground so you could
Be free for two hours only, noted by me, not you.
An Easter Saturday almost gone astray

Because you were lost and only six years' old.
And it was you who rescued me, you know.
Among the swings, the meadow and the river,
You took me out of time, rubbed off on me
What it feels like to care without restriction,
To trust and never think of a betrayal.

ELIZABETH JENNINGS (1926-2001)

The Reprieve

Watching the famous eruption of a volcano on Heimaey, Iceland,
which was broadcast live by any number of TV teams,
I saw an elderly man in braces showered by sulphur and brimstone,
ignoring the storm, the heat, the video cables, the ash
and the spectators (including myself, crouching on my carpet
in front of the livid screen), who held a garden hose,
slender but clearly visible, aimed at the roaring lava,
until neighbours joined him, soldiers, children, firemen,
pointing more and more hoses at the advancing fiery lava
and turning it into a towering wall, higher and higher,
of lava, hard, cold and wet, the colour of ash, and thus postponing,
not forever perhaps, but for the time being at least,
the Decline of Western Civilisation, which is why
the people of Heimaey, unless they have died since,
continue to dwell unmolested by cameras
in their dapper white wooden houses,
calmly watering in the afternoon
the lettuce in their gardens, which, thanks to the blackened soil,
has grown simply enormous, and for the time being at least,
fails to show any signs of impending disaster.

HANS MAGNUS ENZENSBERGER (*b.* 1929)
translated from the German by the author

The night before release

I will put in my case the ready laugh that bubbles from a lover's
  smile...
I will put in my case the drowsy dawn of a virgin sunrise
I will put in my case a bladdered newt with its tiny glass of Ouzo
I will put in my case a tidy row of hard-clogged centipedes Morris
  dancing all their way to hell
I will put in my case the rich brown, brandied voice of Billie
  Holliday with a tender hand to comfort her when the pain just
  won't be soothed
I will put in my case the acid tang of sherbet dab and Spanish in
  its old yellow tube with bright red writing on
I will put in my case old Armitage Shanks for I have read his name
  in writing on many an ill-spent day
I will put in my case the beautiful ebony woman with the easy laugh
  and wide-boned gait who scrubs at the hospital, clearing off the
  vulnerable remnants from the porcelain of cabbages and kings
I will put in my case the tender love of all my friends who hold
  me in their hearts
I will put in my case the shrivelled ancient skin of my embittered
  grandmother whose leathery carcass must be fitting for a purse
I will put in my case my passion for the mighty sea whose majesty
  has called me more than once to take the plunge and rise again
I will put in my case the fairy ring that nestles at the foot of the
  old Torc waterfall in County Kerry with its feathered greens
  and horse wart
I will put in my case the first tot of Bushmills 17 on a brutal
  weathered night in Donegal
I will put in my case the mischief and smile of my oldest comrade
  and Seannachie, Packie Manus Byrne, and each time that I dare
  to lift the lid I'll hear him cry: Auch! Never let the truth get in
  the way of a good story!
I will put in my case the magic of dragons that fly, the violent blue
  of kingfishers
I will put in my now very large case a fine display of rubber penises
  of every height and hue, a pair of jellied eels with KY tubes and
  rubber lube
I will put in my case a snugly fitting pair of snappy yellow marigolds
  and a squeaky leather cane

I will put in my case a dose of salts for Lot, a pair of scales for
   Solomon, a needle and thread for John the B, an extra rib for
   Adam, a pair of specs for Eve (for she surely needed them) and
   a special word for Lucifer for he's had a very bad press!

There's a lot to be said for medication.

JULIE McNAMARA (*b.* 1960)

A Full Recovery

Oh play that thing!
I'm fit to burst my stitches
With this mad itch
That's yanking me,
Yowls at me,
Hot Bechet blasts –
The Hoot! The Toot!
Tears at my heart,
And I'm up, up and away.
A pop of pain
Sizzles and fades,
But I won't stay tame, stay put,
That can't douse my fires now,
I slither and slide,
Jazzmen devils jolt in my ear,
I won't stop, won't run, won't hide,
I'm gliding wild but smooth so's not to burst,
I'm dancing soft, I can't be heard,
I'm back!
Black petrol swathes of clarinet sound,
(Better than bandages),
Cocoon me,
Roll over me, roll all around,
Slow and low, then gin-streaked shrieks,
My vital signs ignite,
St Vitus fever in my feet,
A growl, a croak, a skip, a beat,
I've flung open the door,
Can't lay abed no more,
I've announced myself to the world anew,
I've quit my hospital pew,
I've run smack back bang into life!
And cawing Creole brass gone mad,
And mutes that wah-wah up on high
Holler – Hallelujah Brother! Yeah Man! Say it's so! –
Let loose their Welcome Cry,
The whole darn-tootin' throb of it
Salutes me,
And I smile.

CLAUDINE TOUTOUNGI (*b.* 1976)

Creative-Writing Session

I walk in out of the rain,
shaking my coat
and scatter drops of daylight
like clear beads
as though, before the door swings shut,
I'll make a last fine flourish of my outwardness.

For there is damage here,
heard in tuneless voices,
seen in each abstracted face that,
subdued to its own pain,
takes my smile of greeting emptily.

With what uneasy shuffling of mind,
pens and sheets of paper
are arranged like place-mats,
for raking out the words
that, too secret for the lips,
might catch the light almost unnoticed
until they gleam like raindrops on the page.

MIKE SHARPE (*b.* 1933)

The Flower

How fresh, O Lord, how sweet and clean
Are thy returns! ev'n as the flowers in spring;
    To which, besides their own demean,
The late-past frosts tributes of pleasure bring.
        Grief melts away
        Like snow in May,
    As if there were no such cold thing.

Who would have thought my shrivel'd heart
Could have recover'd greenesse? It was gone
    Quite under ground; as flowers depart
To see their mother-root, when they have blown;
        Where they together
        All the hard weather,
    Dead to the world, keep house unknown.

These are thy wonders, Lord of power,
Killing and quickning, bringing down to hell
    And up to heaven in an houre;
Making a chiming of a passing-bell.
        We say amisse,
        This or that is:
    Thy word is all, if we could spell.

O that I once past changing were,
Fast in thy Paradise, where no flower can wither!
    Many a spring I shoot up fair,
Offering at heav'n, growing and groning thither;
        Nor doth my flower
        Want a spring-showre,
    My sinnes and I joining together.

But while I grow in a straight line,
Still upwards bent, as if heav'n were mine own,
    Thy anger comes, and I decline:
What frost to that? what pole is not the zone,
        Where all things burn,
        When thou dost turn,
    And the least frown of thine is shown?

And now in age I bud again,
After so many deaths I live and write;
I once more smell the dew and rain,
And relish versing: O my onely light,
It cannot be
That I am he
On whom thy tempests fell all night.

These are thy wonders, Lord of love,
To make us see we are but flowers that glide:
Which when we once can finde and prove,
Thou hast a garden for us, where to bide.
Who would be more,
Swelling through store,
Forfeit their Paradise by their pride.

GEORGE HERBERT (1593-1633)

Sometimes

Sometimes things don't go, after all,
from bad to worse. Some years, muscadel
faces down frost; green thrives; the crops don't fail,
sometimes a man aims high, and all goes well.

A people sometimes will step back from war;
elect an honest man; decide they care
enough, that they can't leave some stranger poor.
Some men become what they were born for.

Sometimes our best efforts do not go
amiss; sometimes we do as we were meant to.
The sun will sometimes melt a field of sorrow
that seemed hard frozen: may it happen for you.

SHEENAGH PUGH (b. 1950)

The Bright Field

I have seen the sun break through
to illuminate a small field
for a while, and gone my way
and forgotten it. But that was the pearl
of great price, the one field that had
the treasure in it. I realise now
that I must give all that I have
to possess it. Life is not hurrying

on to a receding future, nor hankering after
an imagined past. It is the turning
aside like Moses to the miracle
of the lit bush, to a brightness
that seemed as transitory as your youth
once, but is the eternity that awaits you.

R.S. THOMAS (1913-2000)

Everyone Sang

Everyone suddenly burst out singing;
And I was filled with such delight
As prisoned birds must find in freedom,
Winging wildly across the white
Orchards and dark-green fields; on – on – and out of sight.

Everyone's voice was suddenly lifted;
And beauty came like the setting sun:
My heart was shaken with tears; and horror
Drifted away...O, but Everyone
Was a bird; and the song was wordless; the singing will never
      be done.

SIEGFRIED SASSOON (1886-1967)

A Northern Morning

It rained from dawn. The fire died in the night.
I poured hot water on some foreign leaves;
I brought the fire to life. Comfort
spread from the kitchen like a taste of chocolate
through the head-waters of a body,
accompanied by that little-water-music.
The knotted veins of the old house tremble and carry
a louder burden: the audience joining in.

People are peaceful in a world so lavish
with the ingredients of life:
the world of breakfast easy as Tahiti.
But we must leave. Head down in my new coat
I dodge to the High Street conscious of my fellows
damp and sad in their vegetable fibres.
But by the bus-stop I look up: the spring trees
exult in the downpour, radiant, clean for hours:
This is the life! This is the only life!

ALISTAIR ELLIOT (*b.* 1932)

Great Moments

When it rains, and I go over my papers and end up
throwing everything into the fire: unfinished poems,
bills still unpaid, letters from dead friends,
photographs, kisses preserved in a book,
I am throwing off the dead weight of my hard-headed past,
I am shining and growing just as fast as I disown myself,
so if I poke at the fire, leap over the flames,
and scarcely understand what I feel while I'm doing it,
is it not happiness that is lifting me up?

When I hit the streets, whistling in sheer delight
– a cigarette in my lips, my soul in good order –
and I talk to the kids or let myself drift with the clouds,
early May and the breeze goes lifting up everything,
the young girls begin wearing their low-cut blouses, their arms
naked and tanned, their eyes wide,
and they laugh without knowing why, bubbling over
and scattering their ecstasy which then trembles afresh,
isn't it happiness, what we feel then?

When a friend shows up and there's nothing in the house,
but my girl brings forth anchovies, ham, and cheese,
olives and crab and two bottles of white wine,
and I assist at the miracle – knowing it's all on credit –
and I don't want to worry about having to pay for it,
and we drink and babble like there's no tomorrow,
and my friend is well off and he figures we are too,
and maybe we are, laughing at death that way,
isn't that happiness which suddenly breaks through?

When I wake up, I stay stretched out
by the open balcony. And dawn comes: the birds
trill sweetly in their heathen arabics;
and I ought to get up, but I don't;
and looking up I watch the rippling light of the sea
dancing on the ceiling, prism of its mother-of-pearl,
and I go on lying there and nothing matters a damn –
don't I annihilate time? And save myself from terror?
Isn't it happiness that comes with the dawn?

When I go to the market, I look at the nectarines
and work my jaws at the sight of the plump cherries,
the oozing figs, the plums fallen
from the tree of life, a sin no doubt,
being so tempting and all. And I ask the price
and haggle over it and finally knock it down,
but the game is over, I pay double and it's still not much,
and the salesgirl turns her astonished eyes on me,
is it not happiness that is germinating there?

When I can say: The day is over.
And by day I mean its taxis, its business,
the scrambling for money, the struggles of the dead.
And when I get home, sweat-stained and tired,
I sit down in the dusk and plug the phonograph in
and Kachaturian comes on, or Mozart, or Vivaldi,
and the music holds sway, I feel clean again,
simply clean and, in spite of everything, unhurt,
is it not happiness that is closing around me?

When after turning things over and over again in my mind,
I remember a friend and go over to see him, he says
'I was just now thinking of going over to see you.'
And we talk a long time, not about my troubles,
and he couldn't help me, even if he wanted to,
but we talk about how things are going in Jordan,
or a book of Neruda's, or his tailor, or the wind,
and as I leave I feel comforted and full of peace,
isn't that happiness, what comes over me then?

Opening a window; feeling the cool air;
walking down a road that smells of honeysuckle;
drinking with a friend; chattering or, better yet, keeping still;
feeling that we feel what other men feel;
seeing ourselves through eyes that see us as innocent,
isn't this happiness, and the hell with death?
Beaten, betrayed, seeing almost cynically
that they can do no more to me, that I'm still alive,
isn't this happiness, that is not for sale?

GABRIEL CELAYA (1911-91)
translated from the Spanish by Robert Mezey

And Yet the Books

And yet the books will be there on the shelves, separate beings,
That appeared once, still wet
As shining chestnuts under a tree in autumn,
And, touched, coddled, began to live
In spite of fires on the horizon, castles blown up,
Tribes on the march, planets in motion.
'We are,' they said, even as their pages
Were being torn out, or a buzzing flame
Licked away their letters. So much more durable
Than we are, whose frail warmth
Cools down with memory, disperses, perishes.
I imagine the earth when I am no more:
Nothing happens, no loss, it's still a strange pageant,
Women's dresses, dewy lilacs, a song in the valley,
Yet the books will be there on the shelves, well born,
Derived from people, but also from radiance, heights.

CZESLAW MILOSZ (*b.*1911)
translated from the Polish by the author and Robert Hass

You Know What I'm Saying?

'I favor your enterprise,' the soup ladle says.
'And I regard you and your project with joy.'

At Grand Forks where the road divides twice over,
the wet wooden squeegee handle poking out
of the bucket beside the red gas pump tells you,
'*Whichever* way – hey, for you they're *all* okay.'

The stunted pine declares from someone's backyard
you happen to be passing, 'I don't begrudge you
your good health. In fact, my blessing – you've got it, now.'

An ironing board is irrepressible.
'Your success is far from certain, my friend,
and still it's vital to my happiness.'

The yellow kernels in the dust, mere chickenfeed,
call out, 'We salute you, and you can count on us.'

We do not live in a world of things
but among benedictions given
and – do you know what I'm saying? – received.

IRVING FELDMAN (*b.* 1928)

Survival Strategies

One Art

The art of losing isn't hard to master;
so many things seem filled with the intent
to be lost that their loss is no disaster.

Lose something every day. Accept the fluster
of lost door keys, the hour badly spent.
The art of losing isn't hard to master.

Then practice losing farther, losing faster:
places, and names, and where it was you meant
to travel. None of these will bring disaster.

I lost my mother's watch. And look! my last, or
next-to-last, of three loved houses went.
The art of losing isn't hard to master.

I lost two cities, lovely ones. And, vaster,
some realms I owned, two rivers, a continent.
I miss them, but it wasn't a disaster.

– Even losing you (the joking voice, a gesture
I love) I shan't have lied. It's evident
the art of losing's not too hard to master
though it may look like (*Write* it!) like disaster.

ELIZABETH BISHOP (1911-79)

Mr Cogito Meditates on Suffering

All attempts to remove
the so-called cup of bitterness –
by reflection
frenzied actions on behalf of homeless cats
deep breathing
religion –
failed

one must consent
gently bend the head
not wring the hands
make use of the suffering gently moderately
like an artificial limb
without false shame
but also without unnecessary pride

do not brandish the stump
over the heads of others
don't knock with the white cane
against the windows of the well-fed

drink the essence of bitter herbs
but not to the dregs
leave carefully
a few sips for the future

accept
but simultaneously
isolate within yourself
and if it is possible
create from the matter of suffering
a thing or a person

play
with it
of course
play

entertain it
very cautiously
like a sick child
forcing at last
with silly tricks
a faint
smile

ZBIGNIEW HERBERT (1928-98)
translated from the Polish by John and Bogdana Carpenter

A patient old cripple

FROM *Life and Turgid Times of A. Citizen*

When I am out of sorts with the things
The world is made of, and box lids
Come off with a jerk sideways, scattering
The little things I can't pick up
Screws and buttons, bits of paper, pencils,
I think how I so loved the world once, as did someone else,
And remember hands that are beautiful – In pictures:
Soft and straight; fingers with tender pink nails;
And hips and legs an advantage, not crisis, in women.
Then I think
To birds my hands would not be hideous
A useful claw (they would see) not white
And strengthless and slabby and straight—so unprehensile.
The hand of my grandchild and mine are the same thing
As a word said differently is the same at root.
I curse the world that blunders into me, and hurts
But know
Its bad fit is the best that we can do.

JENNY JOSEPH (*b.* 1932)

FROM The Kingdom

Over the roofs and cranes, blistered cupola and hungry smokestack,
   over the moored balloons and the feathery tufts of searchlights,
Over the cold transmitters jabbering under the moon,
Over the hump of the ocean big with wrecks and over
Our hide-bound fog-bound lives the hosts of the living collect
Like migrant birds, or bees to the sound of a gong:
Subjects all of the Kingdom but each in himself a king.
These are the people who know in their bones the answer
To the statesman's quiz and the false reformer's crude
Alternatives and ultimatums. These have eyes
And can see each other's goodness, do not need salvation
By whip, brochure, sterilisation or drugs,
Being incurably human; these are the catalytics
To break the inhuman into humanity; these are
The voices whose words, whether in code or in clear,
Are to the point and can be received apart from
The buzz of jargon. Apart from the cranks, the timid,
The self-deceiving realist, the self-seeking
Altruist, the self-indulgent penitent,
Apart from all the frauds are these who have the courage
Of their own vision and their friends' good will
And have not lost their cosmic pride, responding
Both to the simple lyrics of blood and the architectonic fugues of
   reason.
These have their faults like all creators, like
The hero who must die or like the artist who
Himself is like a person with one hand
Working it into a glove; yes, they have faults
But are the chosen – because they have chosen, being
Beautiful if grotesque and wise though wilful
And hard as meteorites. Of these, of such is
Your hope, your clue, your cue, your snowball letter
That makes your soft flakes hard, your aspirations active;
Of such is your future if it is to be fruitful,
Of such is your widow's cruse, your Jacob's ladder,
Of such is the garden of souls, the orchestration of instinct,
The fertilisation of mind, of such are your beacons,
Your breaking of bread, your dance of desire, your North-West passage,

Of such is the epilogue to your sagas of bronze and steel,
Your amnesty, your advent, your Rebirth,
The archetype and the vindication of history;
The hierarchy of the equal – the Kingdom of Earth.

LOUIS MACNEICE (1907-63)

Foundations

When I built upon sand
The house fell down.
When I built upon a rock
The house fell down.
This time I shall start
With chimney smoke.

LEOPOLD STAFF (1878-1957)
translated from the Polish by Adam Czerniawski

Inventory

This is my cap,
this is my greatcoat,
and here's my shaving kit
in its linen bag.

A can of meat:
my plate, my mug,
into its tin
I've scratched my name.

Scratched it with this
invaluable nail
which I keep hidden
from covetous eyes.

My bread bag holds
two woollen socks
and a couple of things
I show to no one,

like that it serves me
as a pillow at night.
Between me and the earth
I lay this cardboard.

This pencil lead
is what I love most:
by day it writes verses
I thought up in the night.

This is my notebook
and this is my groundsheet,
this is my towel,
this is my thread.

GÜNTER EICH (1907-72)
translated from the German by Michael Hamburger

The Way

Thoughtful, hands behind my back,
I walk between the rails
the straightest way
there is.

From behind me
at great speed
comes a train
that knows nothing of me.

This train
(old Zeno is my witness)
will never reach me
for I am always a little ahead
of things that don't think.

And even if brutally
it runs me over
there will always be someone
to walk ahead of it,
his head full of things,
hands behind his back.

Someone like me,
now,
while the black monster
approaches horribly fast
and will never
catch up with me.

MARIN SORESCU (1936-96)
translated from the Romanian by Michael Hamburger

Be Not Too Hard

Be not too hard for life is short
And nothing is given to man;
Be not too hard when he is sold and bought
For he must manage as best he can;
Be not too hard when he gladly dies
Defending things he does not own;
Be not too hard when he tells lies
And if his heart is sometimes like a stone
Be not too hard – for soon he dies,
Often no wiser than he began;
Be not too hard for life is short
And nothing is given to man.

CHRISTOPHER LOGUE (*b.* 1926)

Wooden Heart

My nextdoor neighbor is robust;
It's a horse-chestnut tree in Corso Re Umberto:
My age but doesn't look it.
It harbors sparrows and blackbirds, isn't ashamed,
In April, to put forth buds and leaves,
Fragile flowers in May,
And in September burrs, prickly but harmless,
With shiny tannic chestnuts inside.
An imposter but naive: it wants people to believe
It rivals its fine mountain brother,
Lord of sweet fruits and precious mushrooms.
A hard life: every five minutes its roots
Are trampled by streetcars Nos. 8 and 19;
Deafened by noise, it grows twisted,
As though it would like to leave this place.
Year after year, it sucks slow poisons
From methane-soaked subsoil,
Is watered with dog urine.
The wrinkles in its bark are clogged
With the avenue's septic dust.
Under the bark hang dead chrysalises
That never will be butterflies.
Still, in its sluggish wooden heart
It feels, savors the seasons' return.

PRIMO LEVI (1919-87)
translated from the Italian by Ruth Feldman and Brian Swann

Homeopathy

She told me negativity was bad.
I said it wasn't, not the kind I had.

She told me that the people I resent
will have their own accounts of each event.

She said it wasn't up to me to judge
and that I should examine every grudge

and ask myself if those I cannot stand
are those who hold a mirror in each hand

reflecting back to me the awful fact
of who I am, unwelcome and exact.

She said there was no need to feel a threat.
I said suspicion was my safety net.

I'd allow harmless men misunderstood
if she'd allow the opposite of good.

Of course, she said, malevolence exists.
Respond with anger, though, and it persists

whereas apply benevolence like balm
and often you can soothe the rash of harm.

I did not feel my interests would be served
by spreading peace where it was not deserved.

What about standards, justice, right and wrong?
She said our meeting had gone on too long

and that the remedy that she'd prescribed
right from the start, if properly imbibed,

erodes those thoughts that play a harmful role
leaving what's beneficial to the whole

person (in this case, me). If this is true
then since I did just what she told me to –

taking my medicine, the right amount
at the right time – surely she can't discount

the feelings that remain. She should concede
that these must be exactly what I need

and that my grudge, impassive and immense,
is good for me, in a holistic sense.

I proved my point like a triumphant kid.
She laughed a lot. I gave her sixty quid.

SOPHIE HANNAH (*b.* 1971)

Lessons in Survival

To stay good currency with your heart solvent,
Be a pink bus ticket used as a bookmark,
A maidenhair fern, pressed but eloquent.

Look for a hidey-hole, cosy or dark,
Where no peekaboo finger or eye can excite
A meddlesome bigwig to poke and remark.

Survival is mostly a matter of oversight.
Be an old pencil stub, a brass curtain ring.
Don't keep your lid screwed on too tight.

With luck, your neighbourhood fairy will string
You along as a glass bead, a silver key,
A saved blue feather from a jay's wing.

A person like you, a person like me,
Must contrive to find butter, but not too much jam;
Live happy and warm as a pick-a-back flea.

Don't be a new airport, the flag of Siam,
A battleship decked with bunting and trouble,
A three-volume novel, the Aswan High Dam,

To founder in foundries of smoke and pink rubble,
To swell and topple, absurd, indecent,
To puff and froth like an overblown bubble.

Be a bit too precious to throw away spent:
Be good for others or perhaps a lark.
Be a whispered name, not a granite monument.

PETER SCUPHAM (*b.* 1933)

A Minor Role

I'm best observed on stage,
Propping a spear, or making endless
Exits and entrances with my servant's patter,
Yes, sir. O no, sir. If I get
These midget moments wrong, the monstrous fabric
Shrinks to unwanted sniggers.

But my heart's in the unobtrusive,
The waiting-room roles: driving to hospitals,
Parking at hospitals. Holding hands under
Veteran magazines; making sense
Of consultants' monologues; asking pointed
Questions politely; checking dosages,
Dates; getting on terms with receptionists;
Sustaining the background music of civility.

At home in the street you may see me
Walking fast in case anyone stops:
O, getting on, getting better my formula
For well-meant intrusiveness.
                                  At home,
Thinking ahead: *Bed? A good idea!*
(Bed solves a lot.); answer the phone,
Be wary what I say to it, but grateful, always;
Contrive meals for a hunger-striker; track down
Whimsical soft-centred happy-all-the-way-through novels;
Find the cat (mysteriously reassuring);
Cancel things, tidy things; pretend all's well,
Admit it's not.

Learn to conjugate all the genres of misery:
Tears, torpor, boredom, lassitude, yearnings
For a simpler illness, like a broken leg.

Enduring ceremonial delays. Being referred
Somewhere else. Consultant's holiday. Saying *Thank you*
For anything to everyone.
Not the star part,
And who would want it? I jettison the spear,

The servant's tray, the terrible drone of Chorus:
Yet to my thinking this act was ill-advised
It would have been better to die. No, it wouldn't!

I am here to make you believe in life.

U.A. FANTHORPE (*b.* 1929)

CHORUS: from *Oedipus Rex*, translated by E.F. Watling

Try to Praise the Mutilated World

Try to praise the mutilated world.
Remember June's long days,
and wild strawberries, drops of wine, the dew.
The nettles that methodically overgrow
the abandoned homesteads of exiles.
You must praise the mutilated world.
You watched the stylish yachts and ships;
one of them had a long trip ahead of it,
while salty oblivion awaited others.
You've seen the refugees heading nowhere,
you've heard the executioners sing joyfully.
You should praise the mutilated world.
Remember the moments when we were together
in a white room and the curtain fluttered.
Return in thought to the concert where music flared.
You gathered acorns in the park in autumn
and leaves eddied over the earth's scars.
Praise the mutilated world
and the gray feather a thrush lost,
and the gentle light that strays and vanishes
and returns.

ADAM ZAGAJEWSKI (b. 1945)
translated from the Polish by Clare Cavanagh

Wild Geese

You do not have to be good.
You do not have to walk on your knees
for a hundred miles through the desert, repenting.
You only have to let the soft animal of your body
    love what it loves.
Tell me about despair, yours, and I will tell you mine.
Meanwhile the world goes on.
Meanwhile the sun and the clear pebbles of the rain
are moving across the landscapes,
over the prairies and the deep trees,
the mountains and the rivers.
Meanwhile the wild geese, high in the clean blue air,
are heading home again.
Whoever you are, no matter how lonely,
the world offers itself to your imagination,
calls to you like the wild geese, harsh and exciting –
over and over announcing your place
in the family of things.

MARY OLIVER (*b.* 1935)

In the End

In the end, I want to go away –
I want to speak to the snakes
on Medusa's head.
I imagine
they will give me the truth.

And I'll try to remain calm,
I'll begin with philosophical questions –

I'll ask them why the hero
sings alto, always –
why the hero's voice
never goes deeper than a tenor.

Alto that smells of lilies –
tenor resilient as a green vine –

I'll ask them why
the hero has a woman' s voice.

I was told the snakes are often hungry,
unreachable – for they make Medusa swim
far out into the sea.

I was told the snakes are mute.
Tongueless, voiceless –
Stuck on a bruised head.

But who has ever tried
to listen to them?

In the end, I know
if you let them look
at your face –
they will suck out your poison,
suck out your poison and leave you
closer to your *self.*

SUJATA BHATT (*b.* 1956)

You

Be yourself: show your flyblown eyes
to the world, give no cause for concern,
wash the paunchy body whose means you
live within, suffer the illnesses
that are your prerogative alone –

the prognosis refers to nobody but you;
you it is who gets up every morning
in your skin, you who chews your dinner
with your mercury-filled teeth, gaining
garlic breath or weight, you dreading,

you hoping, you regretting, you interloping.
The earth has squeezed you in, found you space;
any loss of face you feel is solely yours –
you with the same old daily moods, debts,
intuitions, food fads, pet hates, Achilles' heels.

You carry on as best you can the task of being,
whole-time, you; you in wake and you in dream,
at all hours, weekly, monthly, yearly, life,
full of yourself as a tallow candle is of fat,
wallowing in self-denial, self-esteem.

DENNIS O'DRISCOLL (*b.* 1954)

The White Room

Longing for something to be different,
gather it up, jagged with discontent,

carry it to the room of complete whiteness,
white so negative, so generous

it comprehends all colours; a domain
so silent even the smallest shard of pain

falls audibly, relinquishing its hold
like a dead parasite. Take all you've railed

against, the ache of tiny consequence,
love lost, mistaken – and in that radiance

feel it dissolve, as simplifying fire
both cool and warm lets anger, fear, desire

merge with expanded light which, while it's there,
softens even the hardest facts there are.

CAROLE SATYAMURTI (b. 1939)

Reality Demands

Reality demands
that we also mention this:
Life goes on.
It continues at Cannae and Borodino,
at Kosovo Polje and Guernica.

There's a gas station
on a little square in Jericho,
and wet paint
on park benches in Bila Hora.
Letters fly back and forth
between Pearl Harbor and Hastings,
a moving van passes
beneath the eye of the lion at Chaeronea,
and the blooming orchards near Verdun
cannot escape
the approaching atmospheric front.

There is so much Everything
that Nothing is hidden quite nicely.
Music pours
from the yachts moored at Actium
and couples dance on their sunlit decks.

So much is always going on,
that it must be going on all over.
Where not a stone still stands,
you see the Ice Cream Man
besieged by children.
Where Hiroshima had been
Hiroshima is again,
producing many products
for everyday use.

This terrifying world is not devoid of charms,
of the mornings
that make waking up worthwhile.

The grass is green
on Maciejowice's fields,
and it is studded with dew,
as is normal with grass.

Perhaps all fields are battlefields,
those we remember
and those that are forgotten:
the birch forests and the cedar forests,
the snow and the sand, the iridescent swamps
and the canyons of black defeat,
where now, when the need strikes, you don't cower
under a bush but squat behind it.

What moral flows from this? Probably none.
Only the blood flows, drying quickly,
and, as always, a few rivers, a few clouds.

On tragic mountain passes
the wind rips hats from unwitting heads
and we can't help
laughing at that.

WISŁAWA SZYMBORSKA (*b.* 1923)
translated from the Polish by Stanislaw Baranczak and Clare Cavanagh

FROM A Dialogue of Self and Soul

My Self:
A living man is blind and drinks his drop.
What matter if the ditches are impure?
What matter if I live it all once more?
Endure that toil of growing up;
The ignominy of boyhood; the distress
Of boyhood changing into man;
The unfinished man and his pain
Brought face to face with his own clumsiness;

The finished man among his enemies?—
How in the name of Heaven can he escape
That defiling and disfigured shape
The mirror of malicious eyes
Casts upon his eyes until at last
He thinks that shape must be his shape?
And what's the good of an escape
If honour find him in the wintry blast?

I am content to live it all again
And yet again, if it be life to pitch
Into the frog-spawn of a blind man's ditch,
A blind man battering blind men;
Or into that most fecund ditch of all,
The folly that man does
Or must suffer, if he woos
A proud woman not kindred of his Soul.

I am content to follow to its source
Every event in action or in thought;
Measure the lot; forgive myself the lot!
When such as I cast out remorse
So great a sweetness flows into the breast
We must laugh and we must sing,
We are blest by everything,
Everything we look upon is blest.

W.B. YEATS (1865-1939)

FROM Leaves of Grass

Ah poverties, wincings, and sulky retreats,
Ah you foes that in conflict have overcome me,
(For what is my life or any man's life but a conflict with foes,
      the old, the incessant war?)
You degradations, you tussle with passions and appetites,
You smarts from dissatisfied friendships (ah wounds the sharpest
      of all!)
You toil of painful and choked articulations, you meannesses,
You shallow tongue-talks at tables (my tongue the shallowest of any);
You broken resolutions, you racking angers, you smothered ennuis!
Ah think not you finally triumph, my real self has yet to come forth,
It shall yet march forth o'ermastering, till all lies beneath me,
It shall yet stand up the soldier of ultimate victory.

WALT WHITMAN (1819-92)

Invocation

Dolphin plunge, fountain play.
Fetch me far and far away.

Fetch me far my nursery toys,
Fetch me far my mother's hand,
Fetch me far the painted joys.

And when the painted cock shall crow
Fetch me far my waking day
That I may dance before I go.

Fetch me far the breeze in the heat,
Fetch me far the curl of the wave,
Fetch me far the face in the street.

And when the other faces throng
Fetch me far a place in the mind
Where only truthful things belong.

Fetch me far a moon in a tree,
Fetch me far a phrase of the wind,
Fetch me far the verb To Be.

And when the last horn burns the hills
Fetch me far one draught of grace
To quench my thirst before it kills.

Dolphin plunge, fountain play.
Fetch me far and far away.

LOUIS MACNEICE (1907-63)

ACKNOWLEDGEMENTS

The poems in this anthology are reprinted from the following books, all by permission of the publishers listed unless stated otherwise. Thanks are due to all the copyright holders below for their kind permission:

Elizabeth Bartlett: *Two Women Dancing: New & Selected Poems* (Bloodaxe Books, 1995); John Berryman: *The Dream Songs*, © 1969 by John Berryman, © renewed 1997 by Kate Donahue Berryman, by permission of Faber & Faber Ltd and Farrar, Straus and Giroux, LLC); Sujata Bhatt: 'In the End', by permission of the author; Elizabeth Bishop: *The Complete Poems 1927-1997* (Chatto & Windus, 1983), © 1979, 1983 by permission of Alice Helen Meth-fessel and Farrar, Straus & Giroux, LLC; Thomas Blackburn: *Selected Poems* (Carcanet Press, 2001); Edmund Blunden: Selected Poems (Carcanet Press, 1982); Bertolt Brecht: *Poems 1913-1956*, ed. John Willett and Ralph Manheim (Methuen, 2000), © 1976; William Bronk: *Life Supports: New & Collected Poems* (North Point Press, 1977); Sarah Cavill: 'Beginning', by permission of the author; Gabriel Celaya: from *Roots and Wings: Poetry from Spain 1900-1975* (Harper & Row, 1976), by permission of Robert Mezey; John Clare: *Selected Poems* (Penguin, 1990); Wendy Cope: *Across the City* (Priapus, 1980), by permission of the author; Frances Cornford: *Selected Poems* (Enitharmon Press, 1996), by permission of the Trustees of Mrs Frances C. Cornford Deceased Will Trust, via Barr Ellison Solicitors; Stephen Dobyns: *Velocities: New & Selected Poems* (Penguin Books USA, 1994; Bloodaxe Books, 1996), by permission of David Higham Associates and Penguin Putnam Inc.; Gunter Eich: *Pigeons and Moles* (1991), by permission of Suhrkamp Verlag, Frankfurt am Main, and Michael Hamburger; Alistair Elliot: *My Country: Collected Poems* (Carcanet Press, 1989); Hans Magnus Enzensberger: *Selected Poems*, trs. Michael Hamburger and Hans Magnus Enzensberger (Bloodaxe Books, 1994), by permission of Suhrkamp Verlag, Frankfurt am Main; Irving Feldman: 'You Know What I'm Saying', from *The Best American Poetry* (Scribners, 1997), by permission of the author; U.A. Fanthorpe: 'A Minor Role' by permission of the author; John Fuller: *Collected Poems* (Chatto & Windus, 1996), by permission of the Random House Group; Allen Ginsberg: *Collected Poems: 1947-1980* (Viking, 1985), by permission of Penguin Books, Inc.; Ivor Gurney: *Selected Poems* (Oxford University Press, 1997), by permission of The Ivor Gurney Trust; Sophie Hannah: 'Homeopathy', by permission of the author; Zbigniew Herbert: *Selected Poems*, trs. John & Bogdana Carpenter (Oxford University Press, 1991); Elizabeth Jennings: *New Collected Poems* (Carcanet Press, 2002), by permission of David Higham Associates; Jenny Joseph: *Selected Poems* (Bloodaxe Books, 1992), by permission of John Johnson Ltd; Donald Justice: *Selected Poems* (Alfred A. Knopf, 1997); P.J. Kavanagh: *Collected Poems* (Carcanet Press, 1995), by permission of PFD; Philip Larkin: *Collected Poems* (Faber & Faber, 1988) and *The Less Deceived* (The Marvell Press, 1955), by permission of The Marvell Press, England and Australia; Giacomo Leopardi: *Selected Poems* (Princeton University Press, 1997); Primo Levi: *Collected Poems* (Faber & Faber, 1988), by permission of Faber & Faber Ltd and Farrar, Straus and Giroux, LLC; Gwyneth Lewis: *Keeping Mum* (Bloodaxe Books, 2003); Christopher Logue: *Collected Poems* (Faber & Faber,

1996), by permission of Faber & Faber Ltd and David Godwin Associates; **Robert Lowell:** *Collected Poems* (Faber & Faber, 2003), by permission of Faber & Faber Ltd and Harcourt, Inc; **Louis MacNeice:** *Collected Poems,* ed. E.R. Dodds (Faber & Faber, 1979), by permission of David Higham Associates; **Roger McGough:** 'The Death of Poetry', by permission of the author; **Julie McNamara:** 'The Night Before Release', by permission of the author; **Char March:** 'award for bravery', by permission of the author; **Anna Menmuir:** 'We're through', by permission of the author; **Artur Miedzyrcecki:** *14 Poems* (The Windhover Press/University of Iowa, 1972); **Czeslaw Milosz:** *New Collected Poems 1931-2001* (Ecco Press/HarperCollins, USA; Penguin Books, 2001) by permission of Penguin Books Ltd and Czeslaw Milosz Royalties, Inc.; **Adrian Mitchell:** *Heart on the Left: Poems 1953-1984* (Bloodaxe Books, 1997), by permission of PFD (educational health warning: Adrian Mitchell asks that none of his poems are used in connection with any examinations whatsoever); **Andrew Motion:** 'The Middle of Nowhere', by permission of the author; **Pablo Neruda:** *Selected Poems,* trs. W.S. Merwin, ed. Nathaniel Tarn (Jonathan Cape, 1975); **John O'Donoghue:** 'A Prayer to George Herbert', by permission of the author; **Dennis O'Driscoll:** *Quality Time* (Anvil Press Poetry, 1997); **Mary Oliver:** *Dream Work* (Grove/Atlantic, 1986), by permission of Grove/Atlantic and the author; **Cesare Pavese:** *Selected Poems* (Peter Owen Ltd, 1969); **Fernando Pessoa:** *The Book of Disquiet,* trs. Richard Zenith (Allen Lane/Penguin Books, 2001); **Sylvia Plath:** *Collected Poems,* ed. Ted Hughes (Faber & Faber, 1981), by permission of Faber & Faber Ltd and HarperCollins Publishers, Inc; **Sheenagh Pugh:** *Selected Poems* (Seren Books, 1990); **Arthur Rimbaud:** *A Season in Hell,* trs. Wallace Fowlie, *Rimbaud* (University of Chicago Press, 1966); **Theodore Roethke:** *The Collected Poems* (Random House Inc./Anchor Books, 1974, Faber & Faber, 1968), by permission of the University of Washington Press and Faber & Faber Ltd; **Colin Rowbotham:** 'Discharged', by permission of the author; **Nelly Sachs:** *Selected Poems* (Penguin Books, 1971), by permission of Farrar, Straus & Giroux, LLC and Suhrkamp Verlag, Frankfurt am Main; **Siegfried Sassoon:** *Collected Poems: 1908-1954* (Faber & Faber, 1984), by permission of George Sassoon and the Barbara Levy Literary Agency and Viking Penguin; **Carole Satyamurti:** 'The White Room', first published in *The Interpreter's House* (2001), by permission of the author; **Peter Scupham:** *Collected Poems* (Carcanet Press, 2002); **Anne Sexton:** *The Complete Poems of Anne Sexton* (Mariner Books, 1999), by permission of Sterling Lord Literistic; **Mike Sharpe:** 'Creative-Writing Session', first published in *Poetry Review,* 91/4 (2001/2), by permission of the author; **Stevie Smith:** *Collected Poems,* ed. James MacGibbon, (Penguin Books, 1985), by permission of the Estate of James MacGibbon and New Directions; **Leopold Staff:** *An Empty Room,* trs. Adam Czerniawski (Bloodaxe Books, 1983), by permission of the translator; **Wislawa Szymborska:** *View with a Grain of Sand: Selected Poems,* trs. Stanislaw Baranczak and Clare Cavanagh (Harcourt Brace & Co., 1993, Faber & Faber, 1996); **R.S. Thomas:** *Collected Poems 1945-1990* (J.M. Dent, 1993), by permission of the estate of the author; **Rosemary Tonks:** *Iliad of Broken Sentences* (The Bodley Head, 1967), © 1967 Rosemary Tonks; **Claudine Toutoungi:** 'A Full Recovery' by permission of the author; **Sarah Wardle:** *Fields Away* (Bloodaxe Books, 2003); **C.K. Williams:** *New & Selected Poems* (Farrar, Straus & Giroux, USA; Bloodaxe Books, 1995); **W.B. Yeats:** *The Poems,* ed. Richard J. Finneran (Macmillan, 1991), by permission of A.P. Watt Ltd on behalf of Michael B.

Yeats and Simon & Schuster Inc.; **Adam Zagajewski:** *Without End: New and Selected Poems* (Farrar, Straus & Giroux, 2002).

Every effort has been made to trace copyright holders of the poems published in this book. The editor and publishers apologise if any material has been included without permission or without the appropriate acknowledgement, and would be glad to be told of anyone who has not been consulted.

INDEX OF WRITERS

Staying Alive
real poems for unreal times
edited by NEIL ASTLEY

Staying Alive is an international anthology of 500 life-affirming poems fired by belief in the human and the spiritual at a time when much in the world feels unreal, inhuman and hollow. These are poems of great personal force connecting our aspirations with our humanity, helping us stay alive to the world and stay true to ourselves.

'*Staying Alive* is a blessing of a book. The title says it all. I have long waited for just this kind of setting down of poems. Has there ever been such a passionate anthology? These are poems that hunt you down with the solace of their recognition' – ANNE MICHAELS.

'*Staying Alive* is a book which leaves those who have read or heard a poem from it feeling less alone and more alive' – JOHN BERGER.

'*Staying Alive* is a magnificent anthology. The last time I was so excited, engaged and enthralled by a collection of poems was when I first encountered *The Rattle Bag*' – PHILIP PULLMAN

'A vibrant, brilliantly diverse anthology of poems to delight the mind, heart and soul. A book for people who know they love poetry, and for people who think they don't' – HELEN DUNMORE.

'Usually if you say a book is "inspirational" that means it's New Agey and soft at the center. This astonishingly rich anthology, by contrast, shows that what is edgy, authentic and provocative can also awaken the spirit and make its readers quick with consciousness' – EDMUND WHITE.

'This is a book to make you fall in love with poetry…Go out and buy it for everyone you love' – CHRISTINA PATTERSON, *Independent*

'Anyone who has the faintest glimmer of interest in modern poetry must buy it. If I were master of the universe or held the lottery's purse strings, there would be a copy of it in every school, public library and hotel bedroom in the land…I found myself laughing, crying, wondering, rejoicing, reliving, wishing, envying. It is a book full of hope and high art which restores your faith in poetry' – ALAN TAYLOR, *Sunday Herald*

'These poems, just words, distil the human heart as nothing else' – JANE CAMPION